The Denny O'Neil Tapes

A Conversation About Comics, Culture and America, 1970

Edited & Designed by
Walt Jaschek

First Edition, August, 2023 • ISDN #: 9798851474644
Published by Walt Now Studios LLC, 964 Claytonbrook Drive,
Suite 1-B, Ballwin, Missouri 63011 USA. Interview © 2023.

http://waltnow.com

Dedicated to

Denny

Thanks for the stories,
written and spoken

Denny O'Neil at age 31, during a round-table discussion with members of the Graphic Fantasy Society of St. Louis in University City, Missouri, 1970. Photo by Walt Jaschek

Contents

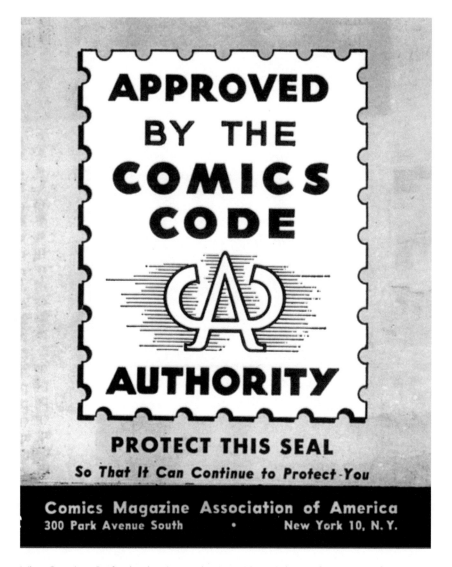

The Comics Code Authority seal, circa 1960. The code is one of many topics covered in this book's round-round conversation. Says Denny of the fate of the controversial code: "It's not going to be seeing its last days. But it will almost certainly be changed fairly drastically…"

On the Cover

Our cover is an enlarged detail from this 1971 DC Comics
"house ad" touting its then recent Shazam Award wins from the
Academy of Comic Book Arts. Illustrations by Neal Adams.

Introduction

By Walt Jaschek

Great conversations linger. Great conversations last.

But great conversations can get lost.

Enthusiastic voices exchanging news, jokes and opinions remain in the memory, and sometimes *only* in the memory, if nobody is around to record what was said, or at least write it down.

Impressions fade, participants pass, and – especially pre-internet – analog recordings disappear into The Phantom Zone. Even early transcriptions can be victims of their own publishing and distribution limitations. (Think limited-run, mimeograph fanzines; we'll get to that.)

But sometimes a great conversation *is* recorded, as audio, and carefully transcribed into text, and published, or at least (as in this case) republished in a place it can be permanently accessed.

Welcome to *The Denny O'Neil Tapes*.

The central feature of this book is a transcription of a recorded, roundtable Q&A conducted in July, 1970 with the late, great comics writer and editor Denny O'Neil – then newly awash in pop culture attention for his work on *Batman, Green Lantern* and more. The hosts and questioners were a small group of comic book fans in St. Louis, Missouri – including me.

I was 15 years old.

The venue was a Sunday afternoon meeting of our local comic book club, The Graphic Fantasy Society of St. Louis, acronym GRAFAN, an affiliation of (mostly) teen-age fans, collectors and gestating creators, gathering monthly. and publishing fanzines *about* the gatherings.

Five of us fans met Denny that day in the home of fellow GRAFAN member Bob Gale, my senior by a couple of years. (Before you ask, yes, *that* Bob Gale: co-writer of the "Back to Future" movies.) Also in the room tossing questions were GRAFAN co-founders Len and Mike McFadden, in their late teens, and a seasoned, much "older" fan, 20something Bob Schoenfeld, publisher of the beautiful, "high-end" zine *Gosh Wow*. Len, Mike and I would end up as editors of the much "lower-end," clubzine *GRAFAN,* named for the club (duh) and printed via hand-cranked, ink-filled mimeograph machines.

Denny, then a tall, 31-year-old St. Louis native visiting from his new, New York home, put the "special" in "special guest" that day. I believe he enjoined at the invitation of the older Bob, with whom he had connected at a New York comic convention earlier that year. The approximately 90-minute conversation centered around what we superhero superfans wanted to know was Going On Behind The Scenes at DC Comics, and was recorded on a portable cassette tape recorder planted in the middle of the room.

The interview would end up as a three-part series in *GRAFAN*, mailed to members, where it was seen by (sigh) dozens. The first part appeared in *GRAFAN* #6, Dec., 1970, where then-editor Mike McFadden "teed up" Denny for readers:

"Born in 1939 with a cheesy cowboy hat on his head in St. Louis, Missouri, Denny O'Neil has progressed to be considered one of comic books' best writers – and worst dressers. He still wears that cheesy cowboy hat.

"His early life consisted of stocking shelves at O'Neil's Market, his family's business; military school; and fantasy. 'Often pinned on a bath towel and played super-hero,' he once said, and at GRAFAN's meeting in July, 1970, he actually looked like Bat Lash.

"He attended St. Louis University, where he majored in English Literature, minored in Creative Writing and Philosophy. From there he left for the Navy, and upon discharge, began a career of drifting that included teaching high school; investigating insurance fraud; a brief stint as a movie extra; and crime reporting.

"It was as a reporter that he wrote a series of articles on comics that won him a pro job in New York. Since then, he has scripted Superman, Batman, Nightmaster, Challengers of the Unknown, Justice League of America, X-Men, Patsy Walker, Adam Strange, Green Lantern *and* Bat Lash. *Just to name a few."*

After lively banter and much laughter with the affable but candid writer, we wrapped the interview, heading *en masse* to the local PBS television affiliate, where the rising-in-popularity writer would appear as guest on a half-hour, face-to-face interview program, name of which lost to time. I remember looking down from a glass wall Green Room onto the sparsely-lit set, thinking the entire day was memorable and magical. In a pure Comic Geek way, of course.

As for those cassette tape, they were hungrily grabbed for transcription. For that purpose, that tape was passed from club execs Len and Mike... to me. Sure! Give it to the kid! He'll transcribe it!

And I did. Twice, in fact. First, in that hot summer of 1970, sitting in my parents' un-airconditioned basement, playing the cassettes on my own little player, hitting "play" and "rewind" hundreds of times until I had what I considered an accurate, text representation of the convo. "Auto transcribe?" "Voice recognition?" The stuff of dreams.

That original transcription will have to suffice as source, because – as I'm sure you are sorry to learn – those tangible tapes no longer exist in my possession. Lost to time? Passed back to the McFaddens? I don't know. Believe me, if I had them, I'd digitize and publish the audio, too.

Instead, in reaction to some comic historians who have reached out looking for the original interview installments in those-hard-to-find *GRAFAN* issues, I've transcribed them again, "taking it from the top" and re-keyboarding while squinting at my few, remaining copies of those inky, mimeograph pages. Collecting all parts in one handy place is worthy chore, I hope you agree, with now, in this format, the opportunity to include scans of select comic pages to amplify the discussion, a technology completely unavailable to 1970 zinesters.

In doing so, this little bit of personal time travel has made me even more cognizant of its passing. Four of the original six people in the Room Where it Happened are no longer happening. Len, Mike, Bob S., and Denny himself have crossed the Rainbow Bridge, sorry to say. I'm more aware than ever we all shuffle off this fandom coil, with or without our zine and comic collections intact. Mimeo ink fades, comics yellow, cassettes get lost.

But sometimes: conversations last.

Walt, 3/3/23

Splash page to *Green Lantern and Green Arrow* #76. This marked
the beginning of one of Denny's most famous and influential
story arcs. Script: Denny O'Neil. Art: Neal Adams. © DC Comics

The Conversation

QUESTION: We've noticed, Denny, that most of your early stories seem to be written in a literary vein, where the script generally doesn't need illustrations. However, your work with Neal Adams seems to be much more visually oriented. Do you write your stories with any visual ideas in mind, and does Adams have much of a free hand in your scripts?

DENNY O'NEIL: Okay, to take your questions one at a time: Yes, I do have strong visual notions. We all do. Some writers like Archie Goodwin go to the trouble of making thumbnail sketches. At the very least, those of us who don't draw have a clear idea in our mind of what the pictures are going to be. There are a lot of good writers who can't write for comics, and the reason? They aren't able to think in terms of pictures: in comics, they're more important than the words. It's entirely a visual medium. Most people who can write comics can write movies or learn to write movies; it's very much the same kind of cognition. Now, about giving artist a free hand, artists always have a free hand with my scripts. It's understood that they can change it. Presumably, and this isn't always the case, they think better visually than we writers do, so if they have an idea for a better picture that tells the story, they're free to change it, and alter the copy so far as necessary to fit the new picture. Some artists aren't conscientious. They put down exactly what you give them in the descriptions and nothing more. Guys like Neal are VERY conscientious, to the point where he will exploit his own creativity in interpreting a story. If Neal or another artist will have a question about a particular panel, he'll telephone. That's easy to do, because we all live in New York. It's the difference between a man who's concerned and thinks of what he's doing as an art form, and the man who's in it to simply get as much money with as little effort possible. So you see, any artist can change the script if he wants. Sometimes I get mad if they change it and it comes out worse, but that is almost a universal given in the business.

Q: Do you visualize your stories cinematically, or in terms of page design?

DENNY: Cinematically.

Q: Do you ever take into consideration page design? For example, we saw some of your scripts that had a double-page spread laid out in thumbnail sketches. Did you take any consideration of page design in that? Did you want the artist to draw it like that?

DENNY: Well, I draw sketches – terrible sketches – when I think the artist might not understand what I'm driving at. For example, if it's a murder mystery, if there is some visual clue in the panel that HAS to be there, I'll sketch it out for him. For example, in *Batman* #225, "Wanted for Murder One: Batman," the position of a pole and a pulley relative to a window is a clue, if you're into figuring these things out, like the "Ellery Queen" trip "challenge to the reader." So for that I did an elaborate sketch so that artist Irv Novick would know exactly how the crime was committed, and how the thing worked. The double-page spreads usually come about when Julie [editor Julius Schwartz] says, "Hey, because of the way the ads have worked out this month, you can do a double-page spread. Why don't you do one?" I love to do it, because it takes about 5 minutes to write on of those big things, and you get paid for two pages. I don't know the script you're talking about, but I suspect it's one where I had some relatively complicated idea, and wasn't used to

For this scene in *Batman* #232, Denny says he "did an elaborate sketch so that artist Irv Novick would know exactly how the crime was committed."

working with the artist, so just in case I put something down. With Neal, and it's getting so with Dick Dillin and Jim Aparo, I wouldn't have bothered. With Dillin, I had to do it a lot at first. He was new to Justice League, and so was I. He's the kind of guy who probably wouldn't telephone, and so I suspect that's how it came about. Usually, you just write at the top of the script, "Pages 15-16, double-page spread," do your descriptions, and add word balloons.

Q: Your work with Neal Adams seems much more visually oriented than with other writers. Do you sit down and talk visual effects with him?

DENNY: No, he talks them out with me. Julie will not let us work "Marvel-style." Or hasn't. Big news, though: we're going to, as an experiment. I'll give Neal a plot: two or three paragraphs. He'll pencil the story as he sees fit, and then give me the artwork to draw the balloons with blue pencil (which doesn't photograph) and write the script on a separate piece of paper. Usually, I'll just submit the script to Julie, he'll make corrections that he feels are necessary, then it's just in the way it works out. I see Neal three times a week, and if he has any problems, we'll sit down and work them out together. The reason my stuff looks better when Neal is doing it is because Neal is a heck of a good artist and involves himself totally. It's a matter of pride with him. He tells at least as strong a story in the pictures as you've told in the words. It's more visual because Neal is more visual, and he cares more. I wish that I could distill Neal Adams and put him in a hypo and stick him in every artist in the business. It's unreasonable to expect that all of them would have his technical skill, his talent, but I'd be satisfied if all of them cared as much as he does.

Q: Why wouldn't Julie Schwartz let you work out the story and art Marvel-style?

DENNY: Well, as I said, we're going to do one. We talked him into it. He felt that the editor had to have control over the final product and wouldn't have the control that he wanted if we did it Marvel-style. I think it's come out [in the press] that he's going to let us do it, because he trusts both Neal and me now. To the best of my knowledge, neither of us have given him a very bad job, or something that needs to be totally rewritten. He's had pretty rotten experiences with writers in the past. So after two years [of working with us,] I think he's willing to let us have a chance with it. The other thing is, there's no deadline. We're going to do this, and schedule it only when it's done. So, if there's some problem, there will be plenty of time to work it out.

Q: Will this be in a regular book, or in something new?

DENNY: It'll be in *Batman,* and features the return of the Joker. It came about because Neal has wanted to do a story set in Steeplechase Amusement Park. It's closed now, but I gave Neal a very dim skeleton of a plot, and he'll work it out.

Q: Do you think this is a better way of creating comics, or a poorer way, or something to give writing a bit of variety?

DENNY: As far as I'm concerned, this is to break the monotony of working the other way. As to whether it's better, in 80% of the cases, it's not. With Neal, with Jim Aparo, it would be okay. Both of them have story sense and are very involved with their work. I remember having big, big problems at Marvel, particularly with the Westerns. You couldn't figure out what the hell the picture was doing there, and you would go to the artist, but he wouldn't know either by that time. It was good in a way: sometimes it forced you to be ingenious and put in plot twists you wouldn't have thought of otherwise to make the artwork work.

Splash page from Batman 252 (previewed in the interview, released in 1973.) © DC Comics

Page 16 of Batman 252 (1973.) Writer: Denny O'Neil. Artist:
Neal Adams. © DC Comics

Q: Gil Kane, in his _Alter-Ego_ interview, said, if I'm not misquoting him, that the only features of any significance in comics have been done by the artists. Do you…

DENNY: This is one of Gil's pet beliefs; he says that all the time.

Q: Do you feel this is due to a lack of interest among writers? Someone like Novick is an excellent artist when working with design concepts. But occasionally his cinematic pacing is hurt because he has a writer who doesn't really care about it.

DENNY: There's more than one question. To start, yeah, a lot of the stuff has been done by artists, and I think I will never be the best possible comic book writer I could be because I can't draw. I believe ideally there should be a marriage of the two. That's what made _The Spirit_ good, aside from Eisner's skills as a draftsman. We artists and writers come as close as we can, and we work as close as we can.

Q: A characteristic we've noticed about books like _The Spirit_ and _Bat Lash_ is that in most instances, the characters were at least consistent from a standpoint of what the characters' personality is and what lines the story will follow through the series, something that both Marvel and National can't always show for themselves. I don't how much effect that has on the reader, but I think in terms of aesthetics, or over a long-term view, consistency like that looks more impressive.

DENNY: I agree. What can I say? The realities of the business frequently make that kind of consistency impossible. For example, Superman is currently being handled by three different editors. They have all made solemn vows to each other that they'll cross-check, and they try. All are men of goodwill, talent, ability. But I'm sure there will be a deadline or something, and they won't have time and there will be inaccuracies. To give you an example, in the *Superboy* that I got the other day (#168,) there's a "Negative Superboy" story written by Arnold Drake, probably back in the Year One. Well, that's going to cause me to change my "Negative Superman" concept that is already in the works, because it'll be too close. I didn't know that Arnold Drake story ever existed. It would have been swell if somebody would have said, "Hey, there's a Negative Superboy story you ought to look at." That sort of thing happens when you're working with six editors.

Q. How are you going to explain to the readers a change in an institution like Superman? Suddenly, as [editor Dick Giordono] did in Blackhawk? I believe he took 3 pages to change the whole thing.

DENNY: No, it's being done very carefully, very gradually, by taking it one step at a time, through several stories. In the first story, we got rid of Gold Kryptonite, White Kryptonite, Purple and Fuchsia and Polka Dot Kryptonite. *[[laughs]]* But at least Green Kryptonite is gone… in a massive chain reaction. No more on Planet Earth. At the same time, though, through a contrivance and a coincidence – which I'm a little ashamed of – we created Negative Superman, which Sups doesn't know about yet. This thing is flying around, gradually draining him of his powers, which we'll show. The first thing to go is Heat Vision, which I always thought was a dumb power. Again, gradually, we're going to increase the strength of Negative Superman, and decrease the strength of our hero. He's beginning to notice it now. In the script that I just finished a few days ago, there's a point where we says, "Wow, I used to be able to do this. What's the matter with me?" So he goes and does the task another way. Eventually, of course, there's going to be a big clash between the two. At this point, I haven't the faintest idea of how we're going to work that out. I suppose it'll take 6 to 8 months, then we'll all agree that Superman is now a manageable character and we can stop doing this and start doing something else. There were a lot of difficulties…

Q. What difficulties?

DENNY: Well, if you noticed, Batman's changed a lot. *[[laughter]]* We're doing basically the same thing with both characters. I think both Batman and Superman have accumulated a lot of unnecessary trimming over the years. They were characters who were equivalent to those automobiles Chrysler used to put out, with tail fins that shoot out as high as the Tower of Pisa, and 15 tons of chrome – unfunctional, too much there to work with. We looked at Superman and Batman from way back, the first issues, and we've tried to decide what made these characters popular in the first place. What is central to both of them? The process is getting to the stuff that I think, that Julie thinks, that Carmine [Infantino] thinks, is getting in the way of telling good, strong stories, and getting back to what the characters are essentially. For example, the powers that Superman has accumulated over the years, I think, make it virtually impossible to give him any sort of conflict short of super-beings from Adromeda-7. Those stories are boring after the 9000th straight issue. Another thing is, the powers are not visual: there is nothing visual about heat vision. Visual means flying around, having shells explode off your chest, crashing through things. I'm convinced that's what made Superman the hit that it was in 1938. Now, if he has all these extreme powers, I can't do that kind of thing and be consistent. So, we want to get him down to a "super man," lower case, not some quasi-God. The third part of the program is to give him some kind of personality.

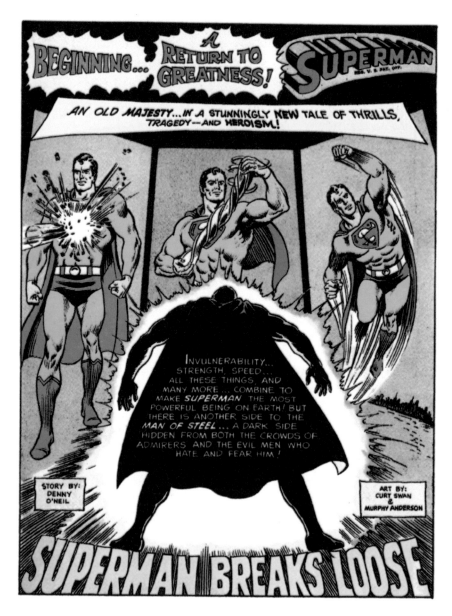

Splash page to *Superman* 133 (1970.) This was Denny's first issue writing the character, bringing about some of the changes to the character discussed in the interview. © DC Comics

Page 8 of *Superman* 133 (1970.) Writer: Denny O'Neil. Artists:
Curt Swan and Murphy Anderson. © DC Comics

Q. I think the same thing applies to television. I remember reading that the reason TV families are always such huge families, instead of having some kind of family planning behind them, is because the more kids you have in your family, there are that many extra plots that can be used in the story. I expect that actually the same was true in comics: the more gimmicks and things you used in comics, the easier it would be to think of gimmicks around which a story could be adapted.

DENNY: Well, there's that, and there's the phenomenon of when you're writing a story, and you've got a problem in the plot, you say, "Hey, why don't we give him such-and-such power, and we can make one interesting story out of it." Unfortunately, though, then, other writers are saddled with that power throughout the rest of the series. A case in point is Green Lantern's ring. It must have seemed like a darn good idea to John Broome or Gardner Fox or whomever did it to make the ring protect him from mortal harm. It absolutely hamstrung later writers, though, because how can you get your reader worried about him when they know that at the last minute, the ring will come charging over the hill and save him? *[[laughter]]* So we got rid of that.

Q. When you say you're finally getting rid of Kryptonite – which sounds great -- is there a realistic way it's eliminated from the storyline, or are we just done with it, or…?

DENNY: Well, nothing in Superman is realistic. There's a kid that came up to me at a convention, and really bawled me out. I hope it's nobody in this room. If so, please step outside. I've been meaning to hit you for a year. *[[laughter]]* He bawled me out for having the "Living Suns" in a Justice League / Justice Society team-up; he said it wasn't realistic. Come on! You've got a guy who can fly seven times the speed of light, and a guy named Superman, and Green Lantern. We're not in the business of social realism, friends. To answer your question, Superman will be realistic the way Tolkien is realistic. We're not simply saying that Kryptonite is gone. I wrote a story around it, and it will be explained within the context of that story.

Q. Are you going to get rid of Lex Luthor?

DENNY: I don't know. We're going to get of the stories, I think, where Luthor takes over some planet and Superman stops there on his way home. I just finished a story that did that, I'm ashamed of it. It'll be in *World's Finest*. I'm trying to restore to comics some sense of awe of inter-galactic distances, and some sense of man's tininess in this universe. Superman stories have been such that even garden-variety crooks have rockets that can blast them out of the galaxy, like you get them at Woolworth's or something. *[[laughter]]*

Q. With National [DC] trying out these new Western titles, I don't suppose there's any chance they might revive Bat Lash?

DENNY: There is a chance! There's no chance of it being featured in his own book; Bat Lash had the worst sales in the whole 30-some-odd history of National Periodical Publications. We're targeting it for a back-up feature in one of Giordano's Western books.

Q: Was [DC publisher Carmine] Infantino as excited about *Bat Lash* as everyone else was?

DENNY: Oh, it was Infantino's baby. He kept it alive three issues after the business office told him he had to absolutely stop publishing it. *[[laughter]]*

Q: We noticed in the Bat Lash book you collaborated on the script with Sergio Aragonés…

DENNY: One of the great men of the Western Hemisphere.

Q: As we understand it, Aragonés just laid it out, and suggested the series.

DENNY: Well, that's the only case I can think of where too many cooks didn't spoil the broth. Infantino sent Sergio a plot idea, and Sergio laid it out on typing paper with sketches very similar to the sketches he does for Mad Magazine in the margins. That was sent to Nick Cardy, who did the polished artwork, then given to me to put in the dialogue and captions. Then it was given back to Nick or whoever was inking it to finish it up.

Q: Do you like working with Nick Cardy?

DENNY: Yeah, sure.

Q: Bat Lash was so much more impressive visually than anything else he's done.

DENNY: It was a labor of love for everybody concerned. We all thought Bat Lash was a great character. It was a chance to do something that only comics can do and the medium has never done. Wil Eisner came close with The Spirit to the sort of thing we were trying to do, but we were trying to go one step past The Spirit. The book was written basically humorously, but we all had very serious ideas about who Bat Lash was.

Splash page from *Bat Lash #6*. Writer: Denny O'Neil. Artist:
Nick Cardy. © DC Comics

Page 2 of *Bat Lash #6*. © DC Comics

Page 3 of *Bat Lash* #6. © DC Comics

Q: And what did you all think of him?

DENNY: We all thought of him as more of a tragic figure than slapstick comedy. He was a poor bastard who was tied, chained and tethered by his own weaknesses, and he couldn't do anything about them because he was too weak to overcome them. He had the makings of a very noble man, but because he was basically greedy and banal, he never exceeded the level of a very pleasant bastard. But he knew that! And he was unhappy about it.

Q: In one story, Bat Lash mugged an old man. Was rather surprised the Comics Code would let the hero of the book not only assault but rob a person.

DENNY: You weren't as surprised as we were. *[[laughter]]*

Q: You were saying in New York that the Comics Code would be seeing its last days soon.

DENNY: No, it's not going to be seeing its last days. It will almost certainly be changed fairly drastically.

Q: Do you know what form the Code will take? Will the company say, "This is our organization, you're going to do it our way." Or just make suggestions? How firm will they be?

DENNY: I don't know. I suspect there will be a committee composed of Infantino, Stan Lee, some people from ACBA (The Academy of Comic Book Arts) – probably the board – and we'll go see Len Darvin and suggest revisions in the Code to liberalize it. What I think is most important is to make it less authoritarian. I have never objected to the Code not letting me get away with various kind of crimes, with not letting the hero do things that are outside the law, as much as the Code forcing me to always make authoritarian figures a cross between Buddha and Jesus. *[[laughter]]* There's a guy at Harvard who developed what he calls an "F Scale." I can't think of his name. Right after World War II, he interviewed a lot of Italian and Nazi officers, and tried to isolate the personality traits of the two, to get a composite of the Fascist personality. I think the Code as it stands – to nobody's fault, particularly – would rate very high on his "F Scale."

Q: There are rules in the Code about the image you have to present of the government. The rule that you have to always present it as a favorable institution seems really… castrating.

DENNY: Not only castrating, but maybe immoral. The Code says, in effect, "anytime you present authority anything less than supernatural authority, it's absolutely infallible. You're committing an immoral act." That's a personal opinion; a lot of people wouldn't agree with it. I feel very strongly that a lot of the mess America is in is due to an excessive reverence for authority.

Q: You scripted all of *The Creeper* issues, didn't you?

DENNY: All but the first one in *Showcase.*

Q: How did you like working with Steve Ditko?

DENNY: Yeah, sure is nice weather we're having. *[[laughter]]*

Oh, Steve is very talented guy, but we disagree in almost every possible
way to disagree, on politics, on morality. So after the second issue of *The Creeper,* I wasn't working with Steve anymore. I was working through Giordano. It was even worse for Steve Skeates, who looks like a hippy, and was doing *Hawk and Dove* with him.

Ditko is very big on Ayn Rand, and, well, *Mr. A* sums up his whole philosophy. He didn't like – I think he didn't like – my version of the Creeper because we had the character sort of self-satirizing in the thought balloons. He made fun of himself, and it's one of Ditko's tenets that heroes have to be serious and straight. I don't think he like the way we handled the character at all. You'll notice that he did less and less work on *Creeper* books as time went on, until Mike Peppe finished the last one.

Q: We suppose Ditko was less than complimentary on the subject of Steve Skeates.

DENNY: I never heard him of the subject of Steve Skeates, but Steve has a beard, shoulder-length hair, wears beads...

Q: Steve Skeates seems to be a very pacifistic guy, and Ditko seems a hard-lined individual. He knows inside and out to repeat it...

DENNY: Have you ever read Ayn Rand?

Q: No, that's the problem. I do know that [in Rand's work] everything is black and white, there's no grey, and if you rip something off from Woolworth's, then you're a hard criminal, where he stands on everything. You have to know his philosophy inside and out to repeat it...

DENNY: Right, sure. [Rand says] anybody who breaks the law is subject to the full punishment. Well, what is never asked is, "Are the laws just in the first place?" Ayn Rand asks it. Rand is badmouthed a lot, but she's not as superficial as people make her seem. She's capable as being interpreted as easy justification for the whole capitalistic trip. I don't want to get into that thing; I'm not putting down capitalism, but we all know it has some evils.

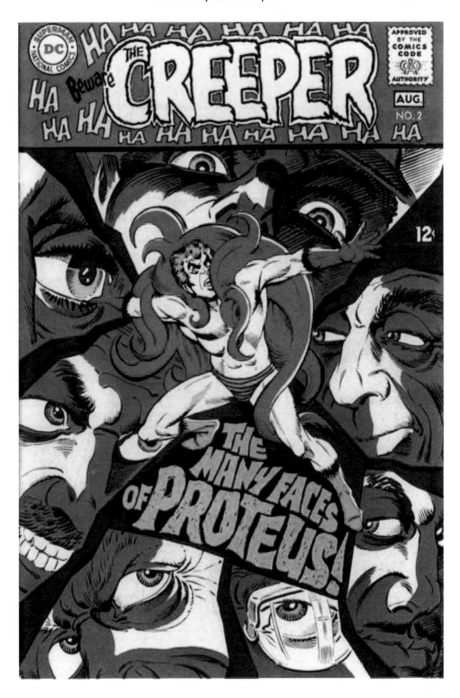

Page 12 of *Beware the Creeper* #2 (1968.) Writer: Denny O'Neil (as Sergius O'Shaunnesy) Artist: Steve Ditko. © DC Comics

You know, somebody like a businessman who isn't terribly interested in philosophy, but might have some small qualms about what he's doing – like exploiting people, or raping the Earth, or polluting the air – can look at Rand and get a kind of justification from it that people get from certain religious sects, which also state that if God loves you, he'll make you rich, and anything you do to get more money means God loves you the more. I don't agree with Rand philosophically, but…

Q: You pointed out that everybody who digs Rand interprets her to their own satisfaction. There are people, in fact, who justify things that are illegal by saying what they are doing is the last act of *laissez-faire* capitalism, because they are selling hot goods or something…

DENNY: Well, the people who sell POT are the last act of *laissez-faire* capitalism.

Q: Well, wasn't going to say that, but that's the example. *[[laughter]]*

DENNY: Oh, sure. (Pot dealers) are governed by the market, by supply and demand. But Steve Ditko interprets Rand in a very authoritarian way. Meaning that the laws, regardless of what they are, are to be obeyed. And that infraction of these laws is cause for the worst kind of punishment that can be thrown at you. That's because if you break these laws, you are a BAD HUMAN BEING – all in capital letters – and we don't want BAD HUMAN BEINGS, do we?

Q: What was the feeling at National between editors, to get back to the questions, about…

DENNY: To get back to the questions! "Philosophy Hour" has just ended, folks! *[[laughter]]* By the way, it should be added to all that that personally I like Steve. I get along with him very well, except when we get together on something professional. Then we're like two cats with our tails tied together and flung over a clothesline. Socially, it's fine.

Q: Did Dick Giordano have any objection to Ditko injecting this philosophy into his books?

DENNY: If so, Dick never talked to me about it.

Q: What is the feeling about National's "duty" quote unquote regarding the insertion of philosophy of *any* kind into their books? Do they feel they have certain responsibilities, or some particular point of view to push?

DENNY: The current thinking is that we should push [social commentary.] And it's showing up in *Green Lantern*.

Q: "It's showing up in the newspapers; but not in the green, as in money." Isn't that what you said recently? That *Green Lantern* is getting a lot of publicity, but not doing so well in sales?

DENNY: Yes, but I thought you meant if there was a policy in the company for or against…

Q: Well, if all it got was publicity, but didn't sell comic books, then maybe something has to be changed. Here I'm throwing in my own thing, but I think young readers go to comic books to escape school. Then they do not want to catch any teaching in a comic book, if they're going to one thing to escape another. Perhaps there is a way of – I don't want to say watering it down – injecting [social commentary] without making it the focal point of the whole book. I'm not

**knocking things like the pollution issue of JLA. I think
there's a place for it on an irregular basis. But wouldn't you
agree the average kid does not want to be lectured to in a
comic book?**

DENNY: Well, if we ever come off as lecturing, then we've failed
in our basic primary doing, which is to be a medium of
entertainment. Those socially conscious books are such that, if
you look at it, you will find we structure it like a comic book story
very carefully. Anybody who likes action and villains getting
whapped is going to get it in those things. As for the social
consciousness: I'm reacting. We're all reacting. I'm desperately
worried about pollution. I've got a four-year-old son who might
not live to be my age, unless we do something about this. If I
were working in movies or some other medium, I would be
reacting similarly. I don't know that it's we want to "preach."
There has been, of course, a qualified change. There used to be a
time when comic never got into anything at all. The difference
now is that if you have a story you want to tell about some social
problem, and you can still make it an entertaining comic book,
you can do it. The only restrictions are that of the Comics Code
and certain editors' hang-ups. Like, the *Green Lantern* I plotted last
night will be pretty much a straight fantasy trip. There will be a
little bow to women's lib to make my wife happy. *[[laughter]]* And
in the last couple of issues, Green Lantern and Green Arrow
have travelled off Earth with a limit of editorializing. And I think
the stories are coming out to be good stories.

**Q (Bob): That's what I was going to say. *Green Lantern* is
coming out very, very, interesting. But I think, however, and
my point was, that too much of this thing can have a
negative effect. When it seems to become a preponderance
of this sort of thing, there is going to be an overt reaction on
the part of the reader.**

Cover to *Justice League* #79 (1969.) Art: Neal Adams and Murphy
Anderson. © DC Comics

Page 8 of *Justice League of America* 79 (1969.) Writer: Denny O'Neil.
Artists: Dick Dillin and Joe Giella. © DC Comics

Page 8 of *Justice League of America* 79 (1970.) Writer: Denny O'Neil. Artists: Dick Dillin and Joe Giella. © DC Comics

DENNY: Well, in the case of Green Lantern, we've got no place to go but up. Nobody's buying the book, anyway.

Q (Len): It seems that the average cretin ten-year-old who is strictly interested in action can still buy the comic and be entertained. This thing is, you can script the book in such a way that he can read it and completely avoid any philosophical points. I assume it's the length of a comic book that keeps you from getting into anything too deeply, otherwise it's going to be a propaganda job.

Q (Bob): I'm not saying that there is going to be an overt negative reaction the first time a kid reads *Green Lantern*. But I think that after a dozen issue of one crusade after another, it will, in fact, appear to the reader that the plot is being forced into a second position to get out this point of view.

DENNY: Well, when *Green Lantern* #76 came out, in one glorious sweep I was accused of being a paid agent of Red China – my wife wanted to know where the extra money was going – and a fascist pig. I don't know what to do about pollution or race problems. So we're not going to propagandize in the sense that we've got a certain point of view we're pushing. It's more like a cry of outrage. It's saying, "These things are bad and they're killing us. They're killing every one of us!"

Q: Well, you show that in the confusion the characters themselves show. They themselves don't quite know how to react, except something, by God, has to be done, and we can't just sit around talking about these things.

DENNY: And in a sense, comic books have been propagandizing in the other direction for so long, that even if we went a little too far, it might have a healthy counter-reacting effect. Comic books have been propagandizing for some of the worst elements in American life for thirty years. Face it! The resolution of problems by strength, the veneration of authority figures, the "my country, right or wrong" attitude. Maybe some of the people in this room disagree with me, but I feel that these are extremely unhealthy attitudes.

Q: Like the fact that the hero will come to the aid of the people in the end, and everybody can take it easy, because the superhero will stop the building from falling on the kid or something. I think a case in point in Superman himself. How are you going to handle that kind of commentary and not bother the distributors about it?

DENNY: Well, Superman is aimed at the ten-year-old kid, so we're not going to get into anything too deeply, actually. There was a letter in [the fanzie] *Focal Point* from a guy named Calvin Dennis. *Focal Point* carried the story of the changes in Superman, because Arnie Katz is a friend of ours. Dennis put me down for changing Superman, a "venerable institution." I suspected I'd get some of that. My answer is that, among other things, it seems to me that it's immoral to have a character dressed in red, white and blue (Judge Hoffman or Abbie Hoffman's colors) going around being invincible and God-like. You know, why are we in Viet Nam? Maybe because people believe certain people are Superman. So I want to keep the character the "action ace of Metropolis," but show some confusion in him, and show that he's able to make a mistake once in a while, of making a wrong judgement, and even misusing his strength.

Q: Will any of this social commentary come up in the Superman stories?

DENNY: Not directly. Well, like the story I just finished for Superman. There's a guy who owns this plantation and won't let his employees leave an island that's about to blow up, because he wants to get the last possible amount of work and money out of them. And he's the villain. If that's "social consciousness," then, yeah. I doubt we'll get any stronger than that. And that was more of an accident of the process of telling the story. We had to have a villain, and it had to be this guy, or else we would have had to tell a different story. When Julie and I sat down to talk about that, neither of us said, "Well, let's show that sometimes employers exploit employees." It just worked out that way. The difference is going to be that those of us working on the books now are… concerned. It's going to be impossible to write a story which has Spiro Agnew as a real good guy Superman defends the ideology of. It's gonna show up like that. Things were a lot different in 1940. The social climate was totally different. The older guys grew up in those years, and we grew up in the Eisenhower years. It's as simple as that.

Q: National recently ran a two-page poll in most of their titles. Do have any knowledge into the background of this poll? Will [the company] set policies based on it or anything?

DENNY: That was done by the Kinney [Corporation] people, and I don't know if they're going to set policies based on it or not. The comic book business as a whole is in trouble, as I suppose everybody knows. Now, one of the reasons we're in trouble is, we don't know who our readers are. We don't know who we're putting these magazines out for. I think that poll is at least an attempt to shine some light into that great chasm of darkness. We know it's not the fans; you people [in the room] are not the typical comic book reader. If you were, *Bat Lash* would have sold a million copies. *Green Lantern* #76 would have sold two million. Seven hundred letters we got on that! More letters than anybody's

Page 15 of *Green Lantern and Green Arrow* #77, demonstrating
Green Lantern's determined self-reliance. © DC Comics

ever gotten on a single issue of a comic ever. And the last I heard, it was dying on the newsstands.

Q: Do the comic companies see their readership as a very transitive audience, a large spontaneous audience, as opposed to us who buy the same titles month after month? We robots? *[[laughter]]*

DENNY: Yes, there's reason to suspect it's very transitive. You know, like a kid will quit reading Superman when he's, at the very latest, 12.

Q: (Bob) Well, then, would it be to their advantage to go either one direction or another? Either build features that would grow with the audience – I don't mean start with a young audience and mature with them but start with an audience that is basically mature already: a high school audience, for instance, that is not going to go through that many changes, and try to keep this readership to where they are purchasing the magazine on a regular basis. OR try to hit a spontaneous audience, make the titles completely spontaneous within themselves, and have cover as dynamic as possible, knowing that the guy who bought it last month is not the guy who bought it this month. And the more "pow" you put on the cover, the more copies you're going to sell.

DENNY: Like naked ladies.

Q: Like naked ladies.

DENNY: Well, I don't know how to answer that question.

Q: Do you know what I mean, though? Dick Giordano, let's say, is putting out a book that will appeal to a fairly uniform audience, where another editor is putting out a book that will appeal to one person one day and another person another day. It seems to me that a company should either go to an all-spontaneous audience or a uniform audience.

DENNY: Well, we're not going to be able to go to a spontaneous audience for a number of reasons, among which are merchandising problems. We can't put comic book out like they put *TV Guide* out, with the point-of-purchase display and that sort of thing. It seems to me that our best hope is to try and build a solid audience. Doing that is going to require some major upheavals. A lot of attitudes are going to have to be changed. The Academy of Comic Book Arts is in business to change the attitudes. First, we have to change the attitudes of the readers — the public — toward comic books. For years, comics have synonymous with the most microcephalic entertainment. And we are going to have to change the attitudes of the publishers…

Q: And the editors…

DENNY: Well, no, you give the editors a good product and they'll get turned on. Julius Schwartz is just a fantastically happy man now. He's bubbly and happy because he's doing science fiction.

Q: Growing long hair, wearing beads… ?

DENNY: Not quite that far. *[[laughter]]* We've traditionally had trouble interesting The Front Office in a particular product. I don't know how it's going to be with Kinney, now that they own DC.

Q: So you're going to have a good time as the comic industry slides downhill, is that it?

DENNY: Well, that could be. We may be on a real Ragnarök trip. The end may be very soon. But I think there are a lot of things that can be done. A lot of business things – things that should have been done ten years ago. But 10 years ago [in 1960,] Superman was good for 750,000 copies, and the money was just rolling in. I guess at that time they didn't see any need to engage in what I feel are very simple, basic business practices that would tend to build an audience and get the magazine displayed. Practices that would broaden the base of the operation, so that if you had a bad year with the comics, you don't stop altogether. Well, obviously, Kinney is good for that, so that's at least one thing that's been done.

Q: If things continue to go downhill for comics from here – if the comics industry continues to plummet – will Kinney give you the opportunity to restructure things and start out fresh, or will you, as you were talking about before, produce something through ACBA and push it to a publisher on a take-it-or-leave-it basis?

DENNY: I don't know. Certainly, one way to go would be to, say, for an editor to be given $30,000, and told to bring out a book, and his profit comes from whatever is left after he has paid everybody. At lot of companies used to operate that way, and in a business sense, it's a perfectly viable motive operation. I think it would hurt quality, though. I'd have to reduce my rates by about ten bucks per page, or it would push me out of the business. The practical effect would be that those of us who have gotten to point where we are getting some decent money in comics – and not too many people do – those of us who make a reasonable, middle-class living, will have to leave the business and do an occasional comic, when you have, like, an opening for two days. It would be the alternative to devoting one's main energies to this field. Because we now ARE able to devote the main portion of our energies to it the product is good – probably better than it's ever been. But that's a very real possibility.

Q: Is Kinney significantly interested in DC to really institute some revolutionary changes in distribution?

DENNY: Sure. They're talking about all sorts of things.

Q: What sorts of things?

DENNY: Oh, there's the package concept; the subscription concept; the bigger-magazines-with-higher-price concept, which would make comics more attractive to retailers. People are talking about paperback book format, and even hard-cover formats. A lot of things are being kicked around.

Q: Would it be possible to go into producing their own cartoons or something as some sort of advertisements? You know, like the Batman cartoons [on TV Saturday mornings.]

DENNY: Well, the problem with that, I'm told, is that television time is enormously expensive, and to buy even a minute of advertising – even on the Superman cartoon show – would cancel out any conceivable profit a comic book might make.

Q: Well, I was thinking more of making the actual cartoons themselves, and actually try to sell them to a sponsor. There seems to be a correlation between the characters on TV and what's selling...

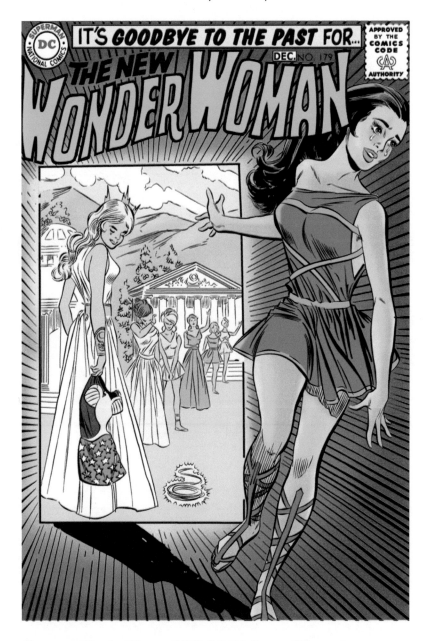

Cover to *Wonder Woman* #179 (1968.) Start of Denny's controversial revamp of the character. Art by Mike Sekowsky and Dick Giordano. © DC Comics

Page 8 of Wonder Woman #179 (1968.) Art by Mike Sekowsky and Dick Giordano. © DC Comics

Page 9 of *Wonder Woman* #179 (1968.) Art by Mike Sekowsky and Dick Giordano. © DC Comics

DENNY: There's not that much of a correlation. That's a big, complicated question that I can't begin to answer. There are licenses and cross-licenses and types of contracts which probably have years and years to run. It begins to be a can of worms at that level, where it takes a corporate lawyer to straighten things out. I agree it would a nice thing if they could do it. Although I really doubt they can. If think it would have been nice if comics would have gotten into the TV and movie business 10 or 20 years ago, when it was possible to get into it. They didn't, so there's no use crying over lost opportunities.

Q: We recently heard Jim Warren [publisher of Warren magazines] was giving up all newsstand distribution and concentrating on some kind of subscription package idea.

DENNY: That's what he told me. As of early 1971, everything will be subscription.

Q: Can he do this successfully?

DENNY: He must think he can! I don't know.

Q: We wonder if he'll get any more subscriptions than the comics used to. They didn't carry very many subscriptions, did they?

DENNY: No, I was told that subscriptions were pretty much a losing proposition even at the higher price. I don't know what Jim Warren has in mind. At the [comic con where we spoke,] he said he was sure he could make it profitable. You know, I hope he succeeds! Like crazy! If he can build an audience, a steady audience, one that is committed for twelve issues at a time, then we can, too.

Q: Right. If he can, anybody can. But how, exactly, will he pull this off? Like, will in one issue he say, "You'd better subscribe if you'd like another issue?"

DENNY: God and Jim Warren know that.

Q: And I suspect the latter isn't too sure. *[[laughter]]*

DENNY: Maybe the former isn't, either. Then again, in some circles, they're synonymous. *[[laughter]]*

Q: That *Gold Key Comics Digest*, considering the different format and display, do you know if that's selling successfully or not?

DENNY: It must do fairly well. I don't know. Gold Key's set-up is so entirely different from any of the other comics companies. What works for them might not necessarily work for anyone else. So, I'm not sure how things are really selling over there. In fact, I don't know anybody from Gold Key, except for Len Wein. One of ACBA's specific aims, one of our many projects, is to bring the people from Gold Key and Harvey [Comics] into the fold, so to speak, to bring about a better and more up-to-date exchange of ideas and information.

Q: Couldn't [DC] possibly do something with printing or production or something to get its comics more widely circulated and more widely recognized?

DENNY: Well, bear in mind that there is an entity called Sparta – World Color Press – and there are commitments to them. I think that this business of printing a half a million copies of every title is one of our big problems. Now, this means you have to sell 275,000 copies to get in the Black. It seems there is an iron-clad audience in this country for 100,000 copies of any comic book –

especially Superman, Batman, Flash, that type of thing. The way the printing is set up now, we have to print those huge amounts. That means they have to SELL huge amounts in order to make a profit. If we could cut that back so that only 150,000 copies got printed, wow! If you could then sell 100,000 copies, you'd be swimming in the black!

Q: Where are all those unsold copies winding up?

DENNY: Mostly second-hand bookstores and the like, with the logos cut off. With both comic and paperback books, all the distributor has to return to get credit is the logo; it's cheaper mailing costs, etc. So we all know what they do. They cut off the logos and dump the things in the second-hand market, selling them maybe 10 for one cent. Then second-hand retailer sells them for 5 cents. What it is doing, really, is stealing from the company. The distributor gets paid for the logos he returns, and then, whatever the market will bear in second-hand retail. And we don't know what to do about that. Science-fiction magazines have a similar problem. According to Ted White, it's what putting *Amazing* and *Fantasic* [magazines] in the red. It's not that the magazines aren't selling, it's that they're not selling in a way that the publisher gets the money.

Q: Sounds like an existential problem.

DENNY: We've got a lot of problems, mostly in distribution and purchasing, and it's going to take a new breed of people – people that seriously care about comic art – to regain the success of the medium.

Q: Denny, on behalf of us all at GRAFAN, thank you very much.

DENNY: A pleasure talking to you guys.   •

Interview First Appearances

The first part of this interview appeared in GRAFAN 6 (1970.).
Cover by Larry Todd.

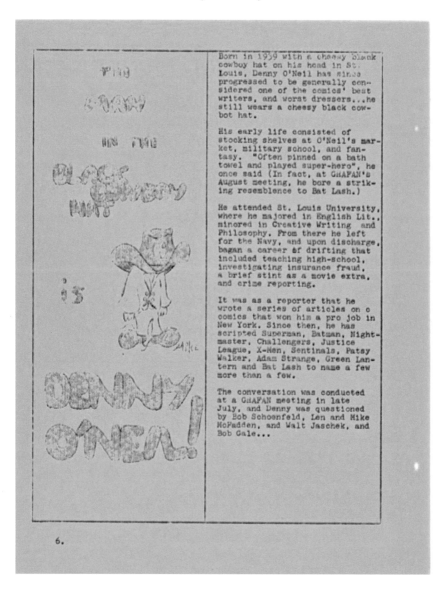

Born in 1939 with a cheesy black cowboy hat on his head in St. Louis, Denny O'Neil has since progressed to be generally considered one of the comics' best writers, and worst dressers...he still wears a cheesy black cowbot hat.

His early life consisted of stocking shelves at O'Neil's market, military school, and fantasy. "Often pinned on a bath towel and played super-hero", he once said (In fact, at GRAFAN's August meeting, he bore a striking resemblence to Bat Lash.)

He attended St. Louis University, where he majored in English Lit., minored in Creative Writing and Philosophy. From there he left for the Navy, and upon discharge, began a career of drifting that included teaching high-school, investigating insurance fraud, a brief stint as a movie extra, and crime reporting.

It was as a reporter that he wrote a series of articles on c comics that won him a pro job in New York. Since then, he has scripted Superman, Batman, Nightmaster, Challengers, Justice League, X-Men, Sentinals, Patsy Walker, Adam Strange, Green Lantern and Bat Lash to name a few more than a few.

The conversation was conducted at a GRAFAN meeting in late July, and Denny was questioned by Bob Schoenfeld, Len and Mike McFadden, and Walt Jaschek, and Bob Gale...

6.

Intoduction to the interview in GRAFAN 6.
Art by Mike McFadden.

The first part of this interview appeared in GRAFAN 7 (1970.).
Cover by Steve Houska and Mike McFadden.

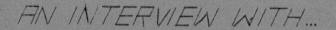

Gimme that again...but a little slower!

w. Houska

DENNY ONEIL

PART II

This candid conversation with the magic Dennis O'Neil was conducted
by a number of Grafan members at our July meeting, which Denny attended as a special guest. The members (even though stunned by con-
fronting a real live PRO) shot questions at the Magic One as long
as his pipe could hold out. O'Neil is no doubt infamous for his
work on a various selection of comic titles, ranging from Patsy
Walker to Challengers of the Unknown, and is especially regarded
for the new quality and maturity he has brought to comix. This se-
ction of the interview continues from part 1 last issue, and is
conducted for the most part by Len & Mike McFadden, & Bob Schoenfeld.

The third part of this interview appeared in GRAFAN 6 (1970.).
Cover by Vaughn Bode'.

Green Lantern 63 (1968:)

The Script

Green Lantern 63, "This is the Way the World Ends!"
Art: Neal Adams

About the Script

In addition to the excitement and fun of being part of this conversation, 15-year-old me had the bravery (or was it audacity?) to ask Denny if he had a script handy for this wannabe writer to study, even briefly.

From a brown, leather satchel he pulled his typewritten manuscript for *Green Lantern* #63 (1968,) "This is the Way the World Ends." The script had been edited by hand (and in pencil) by DC editor Julius Schwartz, another Silver Age treasure. Denny handed it me to keep and autographed it. It's a treasured part of my collection, and a great blueprint for a close-up study of the construction of superhero storytelling, panel by panel, balloon by balloon, coffee stain by coffee stain.

I offer scans of it here for further inspection, interspersing a few published pages to compare with the script; to show how it was interpreted by penciller Jack Sparling; and to detail the attention paid by the editor to all. Reading the typewritten script anew, we see how heavily DC writers of that era were edited – and often rewritten, right there on the page – by the editors, who became *de facto* co-writers in their own… write.

But back to this Hal Jordan *Green Lantern* adventure, a way-out journey one character *in* it calls "a work of pure imagination."

Here's how "…the World Ends…"

Begins.

    – Walt

LOGO: GREEN LANTERN [across top of page)

TITLE: "THIS IS THE WAY...THE WORLD...ENDS!"

SPLASH: DIVIDED INTO THREE PANELS: PANEL ONE, GL MIDDLE DISTANCE,
STANDING ON
THE WEIRD ALIEN EARTH (SEE STORY) IN BACKGROUND. GL TENSE, MOVING
TOWARD READER. LETTERING AT TOP OF PANEL READS: "THIS IS THE WAY...

PANEL TWO: GL, MUCH CLOSER, LOOKING AROUND STARTLED, VERY TENSE.
THE BACKGROUND IS BECOMING "INVISIBLE"--FRAGMENTED, ERASED,
WHATEVER. LETTERING, TOP OF PANEL: ...THE WORLD...

PANEL THREE: GL, VERY CLOSE, LOOKING FRIGHTENED, DESPERATE, FISTS
& TEETH CLENCHED, ETC. STANDING IN A FIELD OF WHITE SPACE...
NOTHING BUT PULP PAPER AROUND HIM. LETTERING, VERY BIG AT TOP OF
PANEL: ...ENDS!"

BOTTOM   BLURB: Suddenly--there is nothing! Without warning, ~~the~~ Green
Lantern is snatched away from ~~the~~ comfortable, familiar surroundings
~~of~~ and marooned in an alien place...a terrifying place...knowing
only that he has but a few hours to ~~solve the mystery--a mystery~~
~~upon which hangs the fate of mankind~~ vanquish a ~~threat~~ which threatens to
doom~~s~~ mankind to ~~certain~~ oblivion!

CREDITS: ~~Story by Sergius O'Shaugnessy~~
          ~~Art by (ARTIST)~~

FOR GREEN LANTERN #63, SEPT. 1968

layout

shorter splash - page size [for indicia)

Splash page to *Green Lantern* #63 (1968.) Script by Denny O'Neil, art by Jack Sparling and Sid Green. Compare this finished page to the concept sketch Denny included on page 1 of his script on previous page. © DC Comics

(handwritten at top: The brother of Hal Jordan -- with Sue -- and baby Howard / refer to Green Lantern #53 -- 2nd story - Pages 2 & 3, etc. / 9 + 10)

1 - HAL, WEARING COAT, AN OVERNIGHT BAG NEARBY, IN FOYER OF NICE
HOME, SHAKING HANDS WITH HIS BROTHER JIM, GETTING KISSED ON THE
CHEEK BY WIFE (JIM'S) SUE, WHO IS HOLDING THEIR ONE YEAR OLD KID.

CAPTION: ~~It begins happily...~~ *Though* Tragedy and terror loom less than
an hour away, ~~But~~ *we begin on a happy note* as HAL JORDAN enters the home of his brother JIM...
~~JIM, he is happy...~~

JIM: ~~XREX~~ HAL! Good to see you, boy! What brings the wandering
insurance investigator to California⸮?

HAL: You didn't think I'd miss my godson's FIRST BIRTHDAY, did you?

SUE: I'm SO glad to see you--and so is little HOWARD!

2 - THE SMILING QUARTET: HAL BOUNCING LITTLE HOWARD.

HAL: How've you all been?

SUE: Fine--except that I STILL can't get this stubborn husband of mine
to admit that he's ~~the~~ GREEN LANTERN!

JIM: Sue, I've told you a ~~T~~HOUSAND TIMES that...

HAL: (2nd balloon) ~~Hey--~~ WHOA⸜ --

3 - HAL, SUE, JIM, HOWARD.

HAL: Arguments I can do WITHOUT!

HAL: (thought) It's ~~irms~~ ironic...Sue's convinced that she married into
~~the~~ Green Lantern's family--and she HAS!

HAL: (2nd thought) Only she's got the WRONG BROTHER!

4 - THEY'RE SITTING AROUND A DINNER TABLE. BIG CAKE WITH A SINGLE
LARGE CANDLE ON TABLE.

CAPTION: A ~~huge~~ *festive* dinner, and many laughs, later...

SUE: Maybe Uncle Hal had better help Howard blow out his birthday candle!

HAL: Glad to ~~be of service,~~ Sue! C'mon, Howie, let's huff, and puff...

5 - HAL BLOWING OUT CANDLE. SOMETHING TRICKY WITH THE ART HERE,
LIKE MAYBE A BLACK AURA SURROUNDING HAL, THE OTHERS WAVERING,
DISTORTED, IN SOME SORT OF PASTEL SHADOW.

HAL: ...and blow--!

CAPTION: It happens, then! As the tiny flame ~~flickers~~ *wavers and* fades,
a chill siezes Hal...

Green Lantern #62, page 3.

THREE PANEL SEQUENCE ACROSS TOP OF PAGE:

PANEL ONE: HAL IS IN SAME SITTING POSITION, BUT NO CHAIR, OR TABLE, OR ROOM. I SUGGEST THAT YOU USE NEGATIVE STAT HERE--SIMPLE LINE DRAWING OF HAL IN WHITE AGAINST BLACK BACKGROUND.

CAPTION: ...he is engulfed in a ~~darkness far blacker than night~~ total blackness...

PANEL TWO: SAME NEGATIVE DEAL. HAL IS FARTHER AWAY, IS TILTED, HALF SITTING, HALF SPRAWLING.

CAPTION: ...he senses the world dissolving around him...

PANEL THREE: HAL IS TUMBLING HELPLESSLY, QUITE FAR AWAY.

CAPTION: and he is falling...tumbling helplessly through a void...

4 - HAL, IN NORMAL COLOR, HANDS OUTFLUNG, FALLING THRU BLACK. THE RING, SEMI- ~~BARELY~~ VISIBLE, GLOWING ON HIS FINGER.

CAPTION: Numbly, his mind struggles to understand...to formulate some plan of action, when suddenly, ~~But before he can marshall his thoughts,~~ a dull, green glow appears on his hand, as ~~and the~~ power ring of ~~the~~ Green Lantern f shimmers into visibility, and ~~from it,~~ emits a far-off ~~he hears a distant,~~ strangled voice...

JAGGED BALLOON FROM RING: Hear me, Green Lantern of Earth... ~~Unless you~~ vanquish GRACCHUS, or mankind is doomed! You must act before...

5 - HAL, STILL IN VOID, CLUTCHING RING HAND, SPEAKING TO RING.

HAL: Before WHAT?! Who are you--? Who's speaking...?

6 - HAL, EXACT SAME POSTURE, EXCEPT THAT NOW HE'S IN A "REAL" WORLD, RECOGNIZABLE SHAPES BEHIND HIM, LIGHT, ETC.

~~HAL: WHO--?~~ [no dialogue]

Bottom CAPTION: Abruptly, Hal stops falling! ~~He finds anit~~ solid ground appears beneath his feet! ~~The ring is silent.~~ A soft ~~distant~~ sigh of wind, nothing more, punctuates the silence...

1 - HAL/GREEN LANTERN STANDING ALONE IN A STRANGE WORLD. BEHIND HIM, AN UGLY PLANT'S TENDRILS ARE REACHING FOR HIM. A RAY FROM THE RING IS TRANSFORMING HIM TO GL--HALF HIS CLOTHES ARE HAL'S, HALF THE GL GETUP.

GL: (thought) I don't know where I am...or WHY! But ~~stxxwhxtxhappenedi~~ ~~mkxismxixxx~~Hal Jordan had better retire until I learn ~~know~~ what's up!

GL: (2nd thought) I'll will the ring to ditch Hal's clothes and let have a look...
G̲R̲E̲E̲N̲ ̲L̲A̲N̲T̲E̲R̲N̲

2 - RING SURROUNDING GL WITH ~~TRANSPARENT ARMOR~~ glowing aura. THE PLANT, NOW OPEN LIKE A MOUTH, TRYING TO GOBBLE HIM.

GL: ~~XXX:~~ Uunh--!

GL: (thought) The ring acts automatically to protect me from ~~danger--~~ mortal harm and I'm beginning to think it'll be kept pretty busy!

GL: (thought, 2nd) That CARNIVOROUS PLANT ~~would've finished an~~ will have to look elsewhere ~~ordinary man in SECONDS--and it'd be an unpleasant way to die!~~ to satisfy its hunger!

3 - GL STANDING ALONE IN THE WIERDEST SETTING YOU CAN DRAW.

GL: (thought) This ~~was an~~ eerie place! ~~It~~ looks oddly FAMILIAR,-- ~~and at the same time ALIEN...~~

GL: (2nd thought) ...like meeting an old man you haven't seen for twenty years!

GL: (3rd thought) I can't DO anything until I understand what happened! And for THAT I need help--!

4 - GL. CAPSULE SHAPED THINGISES SHOOTING UP FROM RING.

GL: (thought) I'll send a quick SOS to the OTHER Green Lanterns...*

CAPTION: ~~(not at top) Capsules of thought-energy pulse from the ring...~~

CAPTION AT BOTTOM: ~~*Note:~~ *EDITOR'S NOTE! There are DOZENS of ~~Green Lanterns~~ EMERALD CRUSADERS throughout the universe, ~~put on virtually every inhabited planet~~ delegated by the ~~mysterious~~ GUARDIANS to maintain law and justice!

5 - THE GREEN CAPSULES IN SPACE, SHOOTING INTO THE DISTANCE.

CAPTION: ...bearing GL's message ~~with a speed much greater than that of light...~~ at multi-light speed...

6 - CAPSULES RETURNING TO GL & RING.

CAPTION: ...and, a heartbeat later, they return--unanswered!

GL: (thought) This can only mean that my fellow GLs have all VANISHED!

GL: (thought) But...HOW? How can a group of highly intelligent,
highly trained ~~creatures~~ gladiators--each equipped with the finest weapon
ever devised...

GL: (thought)...~~how can they~~ disappear without a trace?

2 - GL FLYING.

GL: (thought) ~~IF~~ If ANYONE knows the answer, it's the GUARDIANS!
I have no idea where their home planet OA is in relation to
here...

3 - GL IN SPACE.

GL: (thought) ...because I have ~~k~~ no idea where HERE is! But
I can command the ring to home in on ~~the Guardians central~~ Oa's
segment of space!

4 - GL IN SPACE LOOKING AT STAR CLUSTERS.

GL: (thought) ~~Funny~~ strange...I recognize a FEW of the star clusters!
that's BETA MINOR--~~but~~ and BETA MAJOR should be next...

GL: (thought) ...~~and~~ but instead, there's only a bright NOVA!

5 - GL STOPPING IN MID SPACE.

GL: (thought) I'm STOPPING ~~stopping~~ in the middle of nothing--!
How could the ring DISOBEY? I ordered it to take me to Oa! Why
HASN'T it--?

6 - GL REALLY HORRIFIED.

GL: (thought) ~~Good Lord!~~ GREAT COSMOS! It must be that Oa no longer EXISTS!
The Guardians...the other Green Lanterns...all GONE!

GL:(2nd thought) Am...Am I ALONE in the universe?

Green Lantern #63, page 6.

GL 6

1 - A LITTLE "GHOST" GIRL APPEARING IN SPACE IN FRONT OF HUGELY
STARTLED GL. SHE'S SKIPPING ROPE.
CAPTION: As if in answer to the Green ~~Lantern~~ GLADIATOR'S unspoken question,
~~there comes~~ a sweet, high song, and a second later, he/sees...

GL: (thought) A little GIRL--! ~~Omixxmmx~~

GIRL: (singing, wavy lines, etc.) Mis-ter Green Lan-tern,
(musical notes)   Mis-ter Green Lan-tern,
                                   Go back to where you were--
                                   Mister Green Lantern!

2 - GL GRABBING FOR GIRL, WHO IS DISAPPEARING-- fading out in distance
GL: Come BACK!
GL: (2nd balloon) Too late! She's vanishing...just as everything
ELSE has vanished! (thought)

3 - OUR HERO, REALLY DISTRAUGHT, HOLDING HEAD IN CLAWED HANDS.
GL: (thought) Can it be that...I'm IMAGINING all this? That I've
lost my SANITY?!

GL: (2nd thought) NO! There MUST be a logical answer! The child
said to go back to where I started...
GL: (3rd thought) ...and I might as well follow her advice! I've
got nothing BETTER to do!

4 - GL FLYING OVER PLANET.
CAPTION: The ring whisks the emerald crusader over ~~anximx~~ the
unimaginable vastness of the cosmos, ~~and~~ to ~~the small~~ a planet which
he suddenly recognizes--e as

GL: (thought) ~~It's~~ EARTH! It HAS to be...the right size and shape,
approximately the right location...
GL: (thought) ...but an Earth barren, unpopulated! What catastrophe
could have caused such total devastation?!

5 - GL NEAR GROUND. Hill looms ahead of him
JAGGED BALLOON FROM OFF PANEL: Help! Please...HELP!
GL: (thought) ~~Someone's calling~~ TELEPATHIC ~~TELEPATHICALLY! The thought waves~~
~~are~~ Telepathic waves coming from behind that hill!
GL: (thought) Thank heaven SOMEBODY else is still ALIVE!

2/3 PAGE!

1 - BACKGROUND, GL CRESTING LOW HILL. FOREGROUND, A NICELY CONFIGURED
LADY DRESSED IN ALIEN DUDS ON GROUND, BEING MENACED BY YELLOWISH, TENTACLES
{HUMAN-YET ALIEN}
{CREATURES,}
MONSTERS, SEEMINGLY MADE OF SMOKE, RISING FROM CRATERS IN THE GROUND.
Part of creatures always attached to craters.

GL: (thought) A woman being attacked--by WHAT? I've never SEEN
                                        THEM
anything like those creatures before!

GL: (2nd thought) It looks like they're made of SMOKE...YELLOW
                              POWERLESS
smoke! My ring is USELESS against them!*

CAPTION AT BOTTOM: *Due to a necessary impurity in its construction,
manufacture, the power ring cannot affect anything yellow!

2 - GL, ON GROUND NEXT TO LADY, FACING SMOKIES, XXXTXXXXXX SLUGGING
ONE.

SOUND: Pwop

GL: (thought) ;Oww!; I expected my fist to go right THROUGH--not to hit
meet with some something tough as elephant hide!

3 - A SMOKY GETTING CHOKE HOLD ON GL FROM BEHIND.-with tentacles

GL: Unnngle! ;ULG;

GL: (thought) Didn't see the one BEHIND me! It's got a grip like
STEEL...choking the life from me--!

Bottom caption: Story continues on ... page following!

GL 8

1 - GL FORCING HIS ARMS UNDER THE TENACLES OF THE SMOKIE, LOOSENING GRIP OF S. ON HIS THROAT.

GL: (thought) It Got to loosen it's grip...before I black out!

GL: (thought) It's not quite as strong as a man in top condition...

2 - GL BREAKING GRIP OF SMOKIE.

GL: (thought)...which I just happen to be!

3 - GL PUNCHING A SMOKIE. OTHERS ALL AROUND. BACKGROUND, TERRIFIED GAL.

SOUND: Wook!

GL: (thought) Too MANY of them to end this little soiree with my fists alone!

GL: (2nd thought) If only I knew exactly WHAT they are--! They don't ever sever their connection with those small CRATERS...

4 - GL UPPERCUTTING ANOTHER SMOKIE.

GL: (thought) ...and THAT gives me an idea! Apparently, my playmates are basically VAPOR...

GL: (thought) ...and dependent on something beneath the ground for life!

SOUND: Skok

5 - GL BACKHANDING A SMOKIE WITH ONE ARM, GATHERING GAL UP IN OTHER.
SOUND: sssssssSWAK

GL: (thought) All I have to do is seal up the holes--!

GL: Take it easy, Miss! You'll soon be out of danger...I HOPE!

Green Lantern #63, page 9 © DC Comics.

1 - GL STANDING SLIGHTLY AWAY FROM SMOKIES. A DOZEN BEAMS ARE
SHOOTING FROM THE RING AT THE SMOKIES' HOLES. GROUND AROUND HOLES
DISSOLVING, RED HOT.

SOUND FROM RING, ALONG BEAMS: zzzzzt

SOUND FROM CRATERS: sssshhhhHHHH

CAPTION: Rays of shimmering radiant heat leap from the ring ~~in~~
~~a dozen directions at once~~ at ~~the~~ Green Lantern's willed command...

INSERT SHOT: GREEN RAY HITTING GROUND, AND THE SOIL--"LIQUID"--
FLOWING INTO HOLE.

CAPTION: ...turning the soil ~~of~~ into molten lava which flows into the
craters, sealing them!...

SOUND: glurrgle

2 - GL & GIRL WATCHING SMOKIES "DISSOLVE."

GL: (thought) It's WORKING! They're dissolving like fog in the sun!

GL: (2nd thought) Could those ~~totally~~ ALIEN life-forms be responsible
for...for whatever's wiped out Earth's population?

BALLOON FROM OFF: (singing, wavy lines, notes, etc) Long long ago,

                                                    Long long ago...

3 - GL WHIRLING. LITTLE "GHOST GIRL" SKIPPING ROPE SEVERAL FEET
ABOVE GROUND. XXXXXXXXXXXXXXXXXXXXXXXXXXXXXXXXXXXX

GHOST: (wavy lines, etc.) Before you were born,
       musical
       notes   The world was torn,

                     Long, long ago...

GL: (thought) I have the feeling that those songs contain some MESSAGE...!
she's trying to TELL me something!

BALLOON FROM OFF, JAGGED, TELEPATHIC TYPE: What are you staring at? wh-

4 - GL TURNING TO ALIEN GAL. GHOST VANISHING.

GL: (~~telepathically~~) Uh...NOTHING!

GL: (thought) Apparently, the little girl is visible only to ME!

GAL: (telepathically) I want to THANK you, Hal Jordan!

1 - STARTLED GL., GAL.

GL: (telepathically) You know my identity?

GAL: (telepathically) Certainly! We HAD to--to bring you here!

GL: (2nd telepathically) Who's WE? Listen, Miss...if you have any explanations, I can certainly use them!

2 - GAL TURNING AWAY.

GAL: (tlphy.) I...I can tell you nothing! You must confer with my father, Gracchus!

GL: (thought) Gracchus! The mysterious voice from the ring said Gracchus I must DEFEAT Gracchus!

3 - GL, GIRL.

GL: (thinks) I feel like a refugee from a monster movie asking -- but will you take me to your father? leader...er, FATHER!?

GAL: (tlphy.) I know not this...MONSTER MOVIE...! My father is near, however! I will direct you!

4 - GL., HOLDING GAL, FLYING OVER WRECKED SPACESHIP. GROUNDED, LARGE! with gun-ports

CAPTION: Soon...

GAL: (telepathically) Our ship is down there!

GL: (telepathically) I see!

GL: (thought) Some sort of SPACE vehicle--! Judging from those GUN PORTS, I'd guess it's a BATTLE CRUISER!

5 * RAY FROM SHIP COVERING GL. AND GAL.

XXXXX

CAPTION: Suddenly--am amber beam ray from the spaceship encases the emerald crusader and his lovely companion...

GL: (thought) We're being pulled toward that port! I could clobber the raygun...

GL: (2nd thought) ...but I'll hold my fire till I see some real danger!

6 - FOREGROUND, A FIGURE WITH BACK TO US. MEDIUM DISTANCE, GL & GAL DROPPING THRU OPEN PORT TO PLATFORM IN SHIP FROM WHICH EMANATES THE AMBER RAY.

FIGURE: (telepathically) Forgive my rudeness, Hal Jordan--or do you prefer to be called GREEN LANTERN?

FIGURE: (2nd telepath.) My ship is large! I brought you to this chamber by the ATTRACTOR LIGHT to save me time! Time is VERY IMPORTANT... to all of us!

GL/M

~ in a human way.

1 & 2 - WE SEE GRACCHUS. MAN, IS HE WEIRD! ∧ OLD, WIZENED, YET POWERFUL.
HE'S SITTING ON A THRONE-LIKE GIZMO, RUBBING HIS HANDS, SMILING
MALEVOLENTLY. *GL close to him*

~~GRAC: (telepathically) Yes, we MUST save time! Time is very IMPORTANT to us, don't you agree?~~

GRAC: (~~2nd~~ telepathically) ~~Yes~~, allow me to introduce myself! I
am GRACCHUS, from the planet ORT!

~~TELEPATH. BALLOON FROM ORT:~~ *GREEN LANTERN:* You seem to KNOW who I am--~~ALL~~ of who I am! *Now how about some explanations--?* *BOTH*

~~2 - GL, GRACCHUS.~~

~~GL: (telepathically) Your daughter said you could explain...~~

GRAC: (telepathically) ~~Of course~~! Your puzzlement is very
understandable! I fear I have sad tidings for you!

3 - FLASHBACK: GRACCHUS' HEAD ~~SOMEWHERE IN SHOT~~ *in front of caption*. SPACESHIPS
BLASTING EARTH.

GRAC./CAPTION: "A few hours ago, ~~Earth~~ *EARTH-- your native planet* was attacked by ~~a convoy of pirate ships!~~ *interplanetary marauders!* ~~Ever~~ Ruthlessly, mercilessly, they destroyed every
living thing on the world..."

4 - STILL F.B. SMOKIES RISING FROM CRATERS. ALIEN SHIPS ABOVE.

CAPTION: (italics) "The radiation from their star-drive engines
reacted with minerals just below the planet's crust to create *the*
vaporous creatures you have ~~undoubtedly~~ already seen..."

5 - GRACCHUS, GL., GAL.

GRAC: (telepathically) Their ~~evil~~ *attack* did not stop with mere DESTRUCTION!
They ~~have~~ SEEDED your world--desposited tiny organisms which will
eventually evolve into ~~MONSTERS~~ *monstrous creatures...*

GRAC: (2nd telepathically) ...causing STRIFE, BLOODSHED and MISERY!

GL: (thought) ~~His~~ *my* mind ~~inside my skull...its PAINFUL! There's~~ *reeling from his telepathic waves-- as if they'd* ~~something~~ UNREAL ~~about his message~~

GAL: (telepathically) Father! Shouldn't you relate the TRU...

6 - GRAC. ~~SLAPPING GAL.~~ *standing up from throne.. holding up restraining hand toward daughter.*

GRAC: (telepathically) SILENCE! You are not to QUESTION me--EVER!

Green Lantern #63, page 12. © DC Comics

1 - GL, ANGRY, GRABBING GRACCHUS' ~~RUBBERY~~ HAND.

GL: ~~(telepathically.)~~ ~~Let her alone, Gracchus—let her alone and~~ GRACCHUS! Do as she says! Tell me the TRUTH!

GRAC: (telepath.) WhA What do you MEAN?

GL: (2nd ~~tele.~~) I mean it won't wash! I mean you're LYING!

2 - GRACCHUS ~~RISING UP, HAND RAISED TO HIT GL.~~ *trying to break GL's hand-hold on him.*

GRACC: (tele.) How DARE you lay ~~your filthy~~ a hand on me, ~~scum~~?

GL: ~~(tele.)~~ Sit down...

3 - GL SHOVING GRACC. BACK INTO SEAT, HARD, REALLY MAD.

GL: (tele.) I said SIT DOWN!

SOUND: whoomp

4 - GL, MAD AS HELL.

GL: ~~(tele.)~~ How stupid do you think I AM? You come here with a trumped-up battle ship pretending to be peaceful! You feed me a ~~cock-and-bull~~ story about ~~PIRATES~~ *marauders*...

GL: (2nd ~~tele~~) ..~~pirates~~ *marauders* my ring would've ~~WARNED me about~~ *detected,* had they existed! You don't even bother to TRY explaining why I--of all the ~~men on Earth~~ *EARTHLINGS*--was spared...

5 - LONG SHOT OF THE THREESOME.

GL: (~~tele~~) ...or what happened to the GUARDIANS ~~as the~~ *and the* other Green Lanterns!

GL: (~~tele.~~, 2nd) Somebody's committed a crime--the crime of destroying ~~the GUARDIANS -- the GREEN LANTERNS -- my fellow - EARTHMEN!~~ ~~KXXXX the whole DAMN!~~ And that individual's going to PAY--I SWEAR it!

6 - GL GRABBING GRACCHUS BY GARMENT FRONT, FIST COCKED.

GL: ~~(tele.)~~ There's no one left except ME to judge you--so unless you give me a better story, I'm finding you GUILTY! ~~Talk, Gracchus--~~ GL [added] : Talk, GRACCHUS--

GL:. ~~(tele)~~ ...~~talk~~ give me a reason to spare you the fate of Earth or--

GRACC: (tele.) Your threats mean NOTHING to me, ~~Earthling!~~ GREEN LANTERN! But perhaps you SHOULD ~~hear~~ *know* the truth...

START FLASH-BACK

1 - GRACCY'S HEAD IN CAPTION SPACE. MAIN SHOT, TWO SPACE SHIPS SHOOTING AT EACH OTHER.

GRACC/CAPTION: (Italics) ~~Ixdidxnot~~ "Much of what I told you was ~~TRUE!~~ **FACT!** There IS a war--a war that has been raging for centuries--between ~~my home~~ ORT and the neighboring planet ~~Tro~~ TRO..."

2 - SMOKING CRATERS, GENERAL DESOLATION.

CAPTION: "...long ago the SURFACE of our world was reduced to smouldering, radioactive desolation! We were forced UNDERGROUND..."

3 - VERY UNHAPPY FOLKS WALKING THRU TUNNEL, HEADS DOWN.

CAPTION: "...to live as WORMS--never seeing sunlight, never ~~tasting~~ smelling fresh air! We do not laugh! We do not play! We only labor, creating new machines of destruction! Such is our lot that we have come to hate life ~~xxx~~ itself!..."

4 - GRACCY IN COUNSEL CHAMBER, FACING SOME GUYS IN ROBES. G. IS HOLDING A LARGE SCROLL.

CAPTION: "And still, the war continues, endlessly! I am a scientist, a savant! Recently, I went before our high ~~counselors~~ council..."

GRACC: ~~Here~~ I have **here** a plan for ending our conflict with ~~Tro~~--a plan to finally SETTLE our ancient differences! (TRO)

5 - COUNSEL MEMBER TEARING GRACCY'S SCROLL IN HALF, SNEERING. GRACCY.

COUNSEL: We are not interested in settling our differences! We are interested **only** in VICTORY!

COUNSEL II: You have wasted ENOUGH of our time, Gracchus! Get back to your laboratory, before you completely exhaust our patience!

GRACC: (thought) The FOOLS! The blind FOOLS!

1 - OUTSIDE SPACESHIP. G. IS KNOCKING A GUARD COLD. ~~DAUGHTER.~~

CAPTION: "I did not return to my laboratory! Instead, I ~~knocked~~ stunned a guard...stole a cruiser..."

2 - SHIP IN SPACE.

CAPTION: "...and with my daughter Teira, fled into the cosmos! We wandered among the stars until we came upon a planet like Ort-- YOUR planet!..."

3 - GRACCY IN FRONT OF A SCREEN: ON SCREEN, A ROMAN CENTURION WITH UPRAISED SWORD.

CAPTION: "Using a TIME-SCANNER I devised, I looked into Earth's future, and saw--WAR! I saw ~~the~~ mankind constantly fighting, killing..."

4 - GRACCY TURNING FROM SCREEN, HORRIFIED. ON SCREEN, A MONTAGE: A KNIGHT IN ARMOR, A COLONIAL SOLDIER WITH MUSKET, A MODERN GI.

CAPTION: "...never knowing rest!..."

END FLASH-BACK

GRACCY: Must THIS be the fate of intelligent beings--of ALL beings?
~~No~~.NO...NO! Better that ~~they~~ should never be BORN!

5 - GL, GRACCHUS. NO F.B.

GRACC: (tele) Now do you understand?

GL: ~~(······)~~ Yes...The reason there is no trace of man, ~~nor~~ of the Guardians, of the other Green Lanterns...

GL: (tele) ...is that they do not yet EXIST! We are billions of years in the past--long before history began!

6 - GRACC., GL.

[tele]

GRACC: Exactly! I snatched you from ~~what is, by your reckoning,~~ *your time era* ~~1······~~ to HELP me...to destroy all the tiny organisms which will eventually evolve into humanity! ~~(······)~~

GL: I understand SOMETHING ELSE--that you are INSANE! ~~(······)~~

1 - GRACCY LOOKING VERY MYSTERIOUS, HYPNOTIC. MACHINE BEHIND HIM
PULSING A RED LIGHT.
GRACCY: (tele.) AM I? ~~Am I insane~~ because I wish to ~~spare~~ stop
untold SUFFERING? Look at me, Green Lantern...
(insert: INSANE)

2 - SAME, ONLY CLOSER, AND THE MACHINE LIGHT IS PURPLE.
GRACCY: (tele)...and tell me I am wrong to spare your people their
hideous destiny--the destiny of Ort! Can you say that, Green Lantern?

3 - SAME, VERY CLOSE. ORANGE LIGHT.
GRACCY: Will you use your POWER ring as I ask, Green Lantern? Will you?

4 - VERY ~~DOPEY-LOOKING~~ GLASSY-EYED GL-- as if in a trance.
GL.: Yes!!

Bottom caption: Story continues on .... page following!

1 - GHOST GIRL FLOATING IN AIR ABOVE GRACCY'S HEAD. GL.

GHOST: Mis-ter Green Lantern,

musical notes   The world is a toy,

So full of joy,

Mis-ter Green Lantern!

GL: Huh? You're right...JOY!

GRACCY: (tele) What are you looking at? -- *talking to?*

2 - GHOST GAL, GL.

GHOST: Mis-ter Green Lantern,

musical notes   I'm in your keep,

Don't fall asleep,

Mis-ter Green Lantern!

GL: ~~(tele.)~~ I won't, sweetheart!

GL: (tele.) It almost worked, Gracchus! You nearly succeeded in HYPNOTIZING me! ~~Whoever that child is~~ But ~~that child whoever~~ *someone* reminded me that there's MORE to human life than sadness...

3 - GL

GL: ~~(tele.)~~ ...there's joy, and love, and accomplishment! Maybe we WILL end up fighting one another till we're finally ruined as a people...

GL: (2nd ~~tele~~) ...and maybe we WON'T! In any case, neither you nor anyone ELSE has the right to play God!

4 - INSANE LOOKING GRACCY PULLING LEVER.

GRACCY: (tele.) I will NOT be thwarted! I had hoped to spare ~~the~~ *this* planet, so Teira and I could live here... *with you...*

GRACCY: (tele.) ...but you FORCE me to use my ultimate weapon! ~~DISINTEGRATING GAS~~! At this moment, *DISINTEGRATING GAS* ~~it~~ is seeping from the ship...

GRACCY: (tele. 2) ...a ~~vaporous mist~~ cloud so powerful that it will dissolve the very SUBSTANCE of Earth!

GL 17

1 - XX LONG SHOT: GL FLYING FROM SHIP. A GREY CLOUD RISING FROM BOW.
CAPTION: Without replying, the emerald crusader ~~leaps into the sky~~ rockets out of the ship...
GL: (thought) He wasn't bluffing! Within seconds, that ~~stuff~~ gas
will ~~get into the wind,~~ wind-- be blown ~~backward forward sideways~~ across the
planet!
GL: (2nd thought) Got to get rid of it--QUICK!
2 - GL USING RING. RAY FROM RING IS AROUND CLOUD, PUSHING IT
TOGETHER.
GL: (thought) The ring will push the gas atoms close togebher--
make the cloud a solid mass!
3 - SOLID GREY CUBE BEING BORNE ALONG BY BIG ~~ROUND DISC~~ GRAPPLE HOOK FROM RING.
~~S.~~
GL: (thought) Can't let it touch the ground--it might penetrate
through to the Earth's core! And if I EXPLODE it, we'll be back
where we started...
~~GL: (2nd thought)...with a lot of dangerous particles in the air!~~
4 - ~~RING ON~~ GL IS ~~FORMING A THING LIKE THE FRONT OF A BULLDOZER,~~ CARRYING CUBE INTO STARRY SPACE
~~PUSHING CUBE INTO SPACE.~~
GL: (thought) I'll ~~shove~~ haul it ~~out~~ out of the atmosphere, into
deep space!
[NO MORE HOOK]
5 - IN SPACE. CUBE FLOATING, GL AIMING RING AT IT.
GL: (thought) There! It can't do any harm ~~herex~~ when I...

Green Lantern #63, page 18. Part one of a double-page spread. ©
DC

Green Lantern #63, page 19. Part 2 of a double page spread. © DC

18 and 19 - DOUBLE PAGE SPREAD. SEE ILL-DRAWN DIAGRAM.

1 - ACROSS BOTH PAGES. GL SHOOTING BEAM AT CUBE, CAUSING HUGE EXPLOSION.

GL: ~~xxx~~ (thought) ...~~FINISH~~ BLAST IT!!

~~SOUND: va-KOOM!~~

2 - GL LOOKING DOWN. SPACE SHIP IN DISTANCE. EARTH FAR DISTANCE.

GL: (thought) Gracchus is taking off! Has he admitted defeat?

3 - SHIP WITH RAY GIZMO COMING FROM BOW. GL DISTANCE.

GL: (thought) No..! He's aiming ~~some sort of gun at the planet!~~ one of his weapons at EARTH!

4 - GL FLYING IN FRONT OF SHIP. PULSES COMING FROM GUN. A RAY SHOOTING FROM REAR OF SHIP.

GL: (thought) High-density radiation going ~~toward~~ down...and some sort of ray shooting out into the void!

GL: (2nd thought) ~~I~~ can't worry about the RAY until I skunk ~~his~~ the radiation!

5 - DOUBLE PANEL. RING IS FORMING A HUGE, CURVED SLIDE, WHICH IS TURNING THE RADIATION BACK AT THE SHIP, EXPLODING SAME.

GL: (thought) I'll throw it back in his ~~face~~...and ~~pray~~ hope that TEIRA isn't in the way!

SOUND: zzzip

SOUND FROM EXPLODING SHIP: WRAM

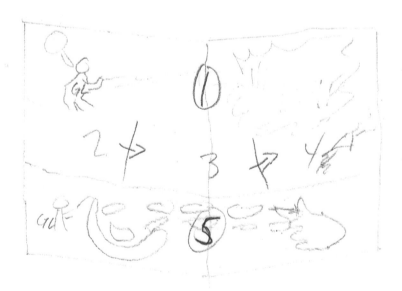

1 - GL. IN BACKGROUND, WRECKED SHIP. ABOVE, HALF FILLING PANEL,
A PLANETOID. (LET YOU IN ON A SECRET...ITS THE MOON ~)- *without craters*)

GL: (thought) . The ship is ~~koelex~~ hopelessly wrecked! No sign of
Gracchus or Teira...

GL: (thought) ~~Good LORD! I understand NOW!~~ *GREAT GUARDIANS! I just realized what* Gracchus was doing with
that other ray...

GL: (thought) He's pulled a ~~mandarin maverick~~ *runaway* planetoid from deep
space into a collision course with Earth!

2 - GL SHOOTING RING RAY AT PLANETOID. BIG EFFORT.

GL: (thought) *No time to ~~whip~~ up enough WILL POWER to destroy* ~~Not even the RING is powerful enough to~~ *the planetoid...* ~~destroy
it...Got to use all my will power...funnel it through the ring...~~

GL: (2nd thought) *But maybe I can stop it short-- swing it* AROUND *the* EARTH-- ~~...force the planetoid to stop to orbit!~~

3 - TIGHT CLOSEUP OF GL FACE *SWEATING* & RING: COULD BE INSERT INTO SHOT FOUR.

GL: ~~(thought) Can't...keep...this up...much longer! My strength
...draining away...~~

GL: (~~2nd~~ thought) I...I ~~MADE~~ DID it! ~~The~~ *Forced the* planetoid ~~has halted~~ *into* ORBIT...

4 - BIG SHOT OF GL HANGING LIMPLY IN MID SPACE. BACKGROUND, EARTH &
MOON.

GL: (thought) ...and unless I'm ~~much~~ mistaken, I've just given
Earth her moon!

TELEPATHIC BALLOON FROM OFF: Green Lantern! The triumph is YOURS!
But at least ONE promise I made I shall keep...

1 - GRACCY &x&&LxIN SPACE SUITX WITH JETS ACCACHED, SHOOTING TOWARD
EARTH. GRACCY XIS HOLDING GAL. GL.
GRACCY: (tele.) ...my daughter and I shall ~~~~~ *end our days* on Earth! Farewell!

GL: (thought) He's moved into the planet's xxx gravity! They'll
BOTH be smashed to a pulp...

2 - GL SWOOPING DOWN BELOW GRACCY & GAL.
GL: (thought) ...unless I get between them and the ground!

3 - GL WITH GAL UNDER ONE ARM, GRACCY UNDER OTHER.
GL: ~~(~~~~~)~~ In a moment, we'll land--GENTLY!
GRACCY:(tele.) So you cheat me even of my final gesture! But
there is one thing you can not take from me...

4 - GL., GAL, GRACCY LANDING.
GRACCY: (tele.) xx ...my death! The explosion injured me beyond
hope...
GRACCY: (tele) ...and I am at last delivered from the terrible
stigma of life!

5 - GRACCY ON GROUND. GAL & GL KNEELING BESIDE HIM.
GRACCY: (tele) GREEN LANTERN— You are a FOOL! You could have lived content with us,
knowing you had performed the greatest possible service...
GRACCY: (tele) ...the service of letting this world remain a barren *land,*
~~rock~~ instead of a place of toil and xxxxxr misery!

GRACCY: (tele) But I take a consolation with me into eternity!
I was bested...by a worthy foe! ~~G...goodbye~~...UNN{...

1 + 2 - GL, GIRL, STANDING OVER GRACCY'S BODY, HEADS BOWED, GAL CRYING.

GL: (tele) ~~his friend...he's gone!~~

~~2 - GL, GIRL.~~

#2 GL: (tele) I'm returning to ~~1964, now~~ *my own time, now, TEIRA!* ~~The power ring can take you,~~
~~too, Teira!~~

GL: (2nd ~~tele~~) I wish you'd come *with me--?* There's nothing here for you ~~here~~ *any more--*

GAL: (tele) But there is! My father ~~was a was~~ was a GOOD
man before...before he became unbalanced! And his ideas were good!

GAL: (2nd tele) I'd like to go back to ORT--to fight for what my
father believed!

3 - GAL IN GREEN CAPSULE FROM RING ~~LEAVING~~ *TAKING OFF FROM* EARTH. GL.

GL: If that's what you want... ~~The ring's beam~~ *My POWER-RING CAPSULE* will take you safely
home! ~~(tele)~~ Good luck! *[added thought]: She insisted on carrying on her father*
GAL: (tele) Thank you...and goodbye! Goodbye...forever! *fight...alone!*

4 - GL SPINNING THROUGH A GREENISH COSMOS, TIME TRAVELING VIA RING.

CAPTION: Wearily, sadly, ~~the~~ Green Lantern wills the ring to bear
him ~~in~~ into the far future, to his own era, ~~in the future~~...

5 - GL TALKING TO GUARDIANS.

CAPTION: ...to OA, home of the Guardians, where, at last, he finds
explanation...

GUARDIAN: So, when our cosmic alarm indicated that someone in the past
was tampering with the foredained march of history, we ~~in~~ *hastily* contacted
you through the ring... ~~and~~ *simultaneously sent out a*
~~and ~~ ~~sent out a~~ psychic energy, ~~a special~~ message
which enabled whoever received it to contact you!

GL: Then, that explains the ~~little~~ "ghost girl"!

6 - GUARDIAN.

GUARDIAN: Yes! We had no way of knowing WHO we ~~contacted~~ *reached,* and we
suspected that ~~they~~ our messenger wouldn't be aware that he--or she--
was being projected back through time!

GUARDIAN II: Her mind received ~~the~~ *out* warning ~~we sent~~ subconsciously!
She undoubtedly spoke it without really knowing why!

1 - LITTLE GIRL, NOT A GHOST NOW, SKIPPING ROPE IN NICE YARD.

CAPTION: At that moment, in a midwestern suburb...

GIRL: Mis-ter Green Lantern,

Mis-ter Green Lantern,

So strong and tall,

You saved us all,

Mis-ter...

BALLOON FROM OFF: ANNIE! Come in now, dear! You've played long enough!

2 - BACKGROUND, ANNIE COMING UP WALK. FOREGROUND, MOTHER TALKING TO MAILMAN.

MOTHER: I declare, don't know how annie's head gets filled with so much silliness!

MAILMAN: Imagination, Missus, that's all it is--just pure imagination!

end

Green Lantern 63, page 63 (1/2 of page.) © DC Comics

Detail from a 1970 DC Comics house ad. Art: Neal Adams.
© DC Comics

About Denny O'Neil

This text is reprinted from the Wikipedia page about Denny O'Neil as it existed of January 1, 2023. It is used with Wikipedia's permission as expressed in its Creative Commons Attribution-ShareAlike 3.0 Unported License, detailed here: https://creativecommons.org/licenses/by-sa/3.0/ Portions are published here for the edification of the reader of this book in an attempt to provide context to Denny's outsized role in modern comic book history.

Dennis Joseph O'Neil (May 3, 1939 – June 11, 2020) was an American comic book writer and editor, principally for Marvel Comics and DC Comics from the 1960s through the 1990s, and Group Editor for the *Batman* family of titles until his retirement.

His best-known comic book writing includes *Green Lantern* and *Batman* with Neal Adams. It was during this run that O'Neil co-created the Batman villains Ra's al Ghul and Talia al Ghul. Some of his other notable work includes scripting runs on *The Shadow* with Michael Kaluta and *The Question* with Denys Cowan. As an editor, he is principally known for editing the various Batman titles. He also sat on the board of directors of the charity The Hero Initiative and served on its Disbursement Committee.

Early life

O'Neil was born on May 3, 1939, into a Catholic household in Saint Louis, Missouri. On Sunday afternoons, he would accompany his father or his grandfather to the store for some light groceries and an occasional comic book.[1] O'Neil graduated from Saint Louis University around the turn of the 1960s with a degree centered on English literature, creative writing, and philosophy. From there he joined the U.S. Navy just in time to participate in the blockade of Cuba during the Cuban Missile Crisis.

After leaving the Navy, O'Neil moved on to a job with a newspaper in Cape Girardeau, Missouri. O'Neil wrote bi-weekly columns for the youth page, and during the slow summer months he filled the space with a series on the revival of the comics industry. This attracted the attention of Roy Thomas, who would eventually himself become one of the great names in the history of the medium.

Writing

Marvel Comics

When Roy Thomas left DC Comics to work for Stan Lee at Marvel Comics, he suggested that O'Neil take the Marvel writer's test, which involved adding dialogue to a wordless four-page excerpt of a *Fantastic Four* comic. O'Neil's entry resulted in Lee offering O'Neil a job. O'Neil had never considered writing for comics, and later said he'd done the test "kind of as a joke. I had a couple of hours on a Tuesday afternoon, so instead of doing crossword puzzles, I did the writer's test."

When Marvel's expansion made it impossible for Lee to continue writing the company's entire line of books, Lee passed as much on to Roy Thomas as he could, but still needed writers, so O'Neil took the reins for a short-term run of Doctor Strange stories in *Strange Tales,* penning six issues. He also wrote dialog for such titles as *Rawhide Kid* and *Millie the Model,* as well as scripting the final 13 pages of *Daredevil* #18 over a plot by Lee, when Lee went on vacation.

O'Neil and artist Neal Adams revived the Professor X character in *X-Men* #65 in one of the creative team's earliest collaborations.

Charlton Comics

The available jobs writing for Marvel petered out fairly quickly, and O'Neil took a job with Charlton Comics under the pseudonym of Sergius O'Shaugnessy. There he received regular work for a year and a half from Charlton's editor Dick Giordano.

DC Comics

In 1968, Dick Giordano was offered an editorial position at DC Comics and took a number of Charlton freelancers with him, including O'Neil.

O'Neil's first assignments involved two strategies for bolstering DC's sales. One approach centered on the creation of new characters, and O'Neil scripted several issues of *Beware the Creeper*, a series starring a new hero, the Creeper, created by artist Steve Ditko. From there, DC moved O'Neil to *Wonder Woman* and *Justice League of America*. With artist Mike Sekowsky, he took away Wonder Woman's powers, exiled her from the Amazon community, and set her off, uncostumed, into international intrigues with her blind mentor, I Ching. These changes did not sit well with Wonder Woman's older fans, particularly feminists, and O'Neil later acknowledged that de-powering DC's most well-known superheroine had unintentionally alienated readers. In *Justice League*, he had more success, introducing into that title the first socially and politically themed stories, setting the stage for later work on *Green Lantern/Green Arrow*. He and artist Dick Dillin made several changes to the membership of the JLA by removing founding members the Martian Manhunter and Wonder Woman.

Following the lead set by Bob Haney and Neal Adams in a *Brave and the Bold* story that visually redefined Green Arrow into the version that appeared in comics between 1969 and 1986, O'Neil stripped him of his wealth and playboy status, making him an urban hero. This redefinition would culminate in the character that appeared in *Green Lantern/Green Arrow* (with many stories also drawn by Adams), a socially conscious, left-wing creation that effectively took over Green Lantern's book to use him as a foil and straw man in sounding out the political concepts that would define that work. It was during this period that the most famous Green Arrow story appeared, in *Green Lantern* #85–86, when it was revealed that Green Arrow's ward Speedy was addicted to heroin. As a result of his work on *Green Lantern and Green Arrow*, O'Neil recounted, "I went from total obscurity to seeing my name featured in *The New York Times* and being invited to do talk shows. It's by no means an unmixed blessing. That

messed up my head pretty thoroughly for a couple of years. ...
Deteriorating marriage, bad habits, deteriorating relationships
with human beings – with anything that wasn't a typewriter, in
fact. It was a bad, few years there."

O'Neil's 1970s run on the Batman titles, under the direction of
editor Julius Schwartz, is perhaps his best-known endeavor,
getting back to the character's darker roots after a period
dominated by the campiness of the 1960s TV series. Comics
historian Les Daniels observed that "O'Neil's interpretation of
Batman as a vengeful obsessive-compulsive, which he modestly
describes as a return to the roots, was actually an act of creative
imagination that has influenced every subsequent version of the
Dark Knight." O'Neil and Adams' creation Ra's al Ghul was
introduced in the story "Daughter of the Demon"
in *Batman* #232 (June 1971). O'Neil and artist Bob Brown also
created Talia al Ghul. During this period, O'Neil frequently
teamed up with his regular collaborator Adams (with Giordano
often assisting on inks) on a number of memorable issues of
both *Batman* and *Detective Comics*. The creative team would
revive Two-Face in "Half an Evil" in *Batman* #234 (Aug.
1971) and revitalize the Joker in "The Joker's Five-Way Revenge!"
in *Batman* #251 (Sept. 1973), a landmark story bringing the
character back to his roots as a homicidal maniac who murders
people on a whim and delights in his mayhem. O'Neil and
Giordano created the Batman supporting character Leslie
Thompkins in the story "There Is No Hope in Crime Alley"
in *Detective Comics* #457 (March 1976). O'Neil and artist Don
Newton killed the original version of Batwoman in *Detective
Comics* #485 (Aug.–Sept. 1979). He wrote a short Christmas story,
"Wanted: Santa Claus – Dead or Alive", for *DC Special Series* #21
(Spring 1980) which featured Frank Miller's first art on a Batman
story.

When Julius Schwartz became the editor of *Superman* with issue
#233 (Jan. 1971), he had O'Neil and artist Curt Swan streamline
the Superman mythos, starting with the elimination
of kryptonite. In 1973, O'Neil wrote revivals of two characters
for which DC had recently acquired the publishing rights. A new
series featuring the original Captain Marvel was launched with a

February cover date and featured art by the character's original artist C. C. Beck. Later that same year, O'Neil and artist Michael Kaluta produced an "atmospheric interpretation" of the 1930s pulp hero in *The Shadow* series. In 1975, O'Neil wrote a comic book adaptation of the 1930s hero the Avenger. A revival of the *Green Lantern* title in 1976 was launched by O'Neil and artist Mike Grell. Reuniting with Adams, O'Neil co-wrote the oversize *Superman vs. Muhammad Ali* (1978) which Adams has called a personal favorite of their collaborations.

Return to Marvel Comics

Upon O'Neil's return to Marvel Comics in 1980, he took on the scripting chores for *The Amazing Spider-Man*, which he did for a year. O'Neil wrote two issues of *The Amazing Spider-Man Annual* which were both drawn by Frank Miller. The 1980 *Annual* featured a team-up with Doctor Strange while the 1981 *Annual* showcased a meeting with the Punisher. He and artist John Romita Jr. introduced Madame Web in *Amazing Spider-Man* #210 and Hydro-Man in #212. O'Neil was the regular scripter for *Iron Man* from 1982 to 1986, and *Daredevil* from 1983 to 1985. During his run on *Iron Man*, O'Neil introduced Obadiah Stane, later the Iron Monger, plunged Tony Stark back into alcoholism, turned Jim Rhodes into Iron Man, and created the Silver Centurion armor. O'Neil's run on *Daredevil* bridged the gap between Frank Miller's two runs on the title, usually with David Mazzucchelli as artist. He introduced Yuriko Oyama during his stint, who would later become the popular X-Men villain Lady Deathstrike. While working for Marvel, he helped write the original character concept for The Transformers, and is credited as the person who named Optimus Prime.

Return to DC Comics

After returning to DC Comics in 1986, he became the editor of the various Batman titles and served in that capacity until 2000.[45] In February 1987, O'Neil began writing *The Question* ongoing series which was primarily drawn by Denys Cowan.[46] Between the years of 1988 and 1990, O'Neil would return to *Green Arrow* writing the *Annual*s alongside the main title. Because he was also in charge of *The Question*, he would appear in all three *Annual*s that he wrote. The *Batman: Legends of the Dark Knight* series began in 1989 with the five-part "Shaman" storyline by O'Neil and artist Ed Hannigan.[47] *Armageddon 2001* was a 1991 crossover event storyline. It ran through a self-titled two-issue limited series and most of the *Annual*s DC published that year from May through October. Each participating annual explored potential possible futures for its main characters. The series was written by O'Neil and Archie Goodwin and drawn by Dan Jurgens.[48] He and artist Joe Quesada created the character Azrael, who was introduced in the four-issue miniseries *Batman: Sword of Azrael* in 1992.[49] That same year, O'Neil wrote the *Batman: Birth of the Demon* hardcover graphic novel.[50] Another DC one-shot issue that O'Neil wrote in 1992 was *Batman/Green Arrow: The Poison Tomorrow*.[51]

Other writing

O'Neil wrote several novels, comics, short stories, reviews and teleplays, including the novelizations of the films *Batman Begins* and *The Dark Knight*. Under the pseudonym **Jim Dennis** with writer Jim Berry, O'Neil scripted a series of novels about a kung fu character named Richard Dragon, and later adapted those novels to comic book form for DC.

O'Neil wrote a four-part column series for Marvel's 1978 *The Hulk!* magazine, under the pseudonym **Jeff Mundo**. "Jeff Mundo's Dark Corners" ran from issue #21 through issue #24 and covered various pop culture topics.

O'Neil wrote a column for ComicMix.

Editing

Joining Marvel's editorial staff in 1980, O'Neil edited *Daredevil* during Frank Miller's run as writer/artist.[1] He fired writer Roger McKenzie so that Miller could both write and pencil *Daredevil*, a decision which then-Marvel editor-in-chief Jim Shooter says saved the series from cancellation.[56] O'Neil encouraged Miller to develop a believable fighting style for Daredevil, and according to Miller, this directly led to his incorporating martial arts into *Daredevil* and later *Ronin*. In the early to mid-1980s, O'Neil edited such Marvel titles as *Alpha*

Flight, *Power Man and Iron Fist*, *G.I. Joe: A Real American Hero*, and *Moon Knight*.

According to Bob Budiansky, O'Neil came up with the name for the Transformer Optimus Prime, leader of the Autobots.

In 1986, O'Neil moved over to DC as an editor, becoming group editor for the company's Batman titles. Speaking about his role in the death of character Jason Todd, O'Neil remarked:

"It changed my mind about what I do for a living. Superman and Batman have been in continuous publication for over half a century, and it's never been true of any fictional construct before. These characters have a lot more weight than the hero of a popular sitcom that lasts maybe four years. They have become postindustrial folklore, and part of this job is to be the custodian of folk figures. Everybody on Earth knows Batman and Robin."

O'Neil said that he saw editing as a support role which should be invisible to the reader, and that if it were his choice his name would not appear in the credits when working as an editor, only when working as a writer.

Teaching

O'Neil spent several years in the late 1990s teaching a Writing for the Comics course at Manhattan's School of Visual Arts, sometimes sharing duties with fellow comic book writer John Ostrander.

Personal life

O'Neil was married to Marifran O'Neil, until her death. He was the father of writer/director/producer Lawrence "Larry" O'Neil, best known for the 1997 film *Breast Men* starring David Schwimmer.

He died of cardiopulmonary arrest on June 11, 2020, at the age of 81. The animated feature *Batman: Soul of the Dragon* was dedicated in his memory. Larry O'Neil wrote a wordless tribute to his father, called "Tap Tap Tap," which was illustrated by Jorge Fornés and published in the *Green Arrow 80th Anniversary 100-Page Super Spectacular* #1 (August 2021).

Awards

O'Neil's work won him a great deal of recognition in the comics industry, including the Shazam Awards for Best Continuing Feature *Green Lantern/Green Arrow*, Best Individual Story for "No Evil Shall Escape My Sight" in *Green Lantern* #76 (with Neal Adams), for Best Writer (Dramatic Division) in 1970 for Green Lantern, Batman, Superman, and other titles, and Best Individual Story for "Snowbirds Don't Fly" in *Green Lantern* #85 (with Neal Adams) in 1971. O'Neil was given a Goethe Award in 1971 for "Favorite Pro Writer" and was a nominee for the same award in 1973. He shared a 1971 Goethe Award with artist Neal Adams for "Favorite Comic-Book Story" for "No Evil Shall Escape My Sight." O'Neil received an Inkpot Award in 1981 and in 1985, DC Comics named O'Neil as one of the honorees in the company's 50th anniversary publication *Fifty Who Made DC Great*.

Appearances in media

In *The Batman Adventures*—the first DC Comics spinoff of *Batman: The Animated Series*—a caricature of O'Neil appears as The Perfesser, one of a screwball trio of incompetent supervillains that also includes the Mastermind (a caricature of Mike Carlin) and Mr. Nice (a caricature of Archie Goodwin). The Perfesser is depicted as a tall, pipe-smoking genius who often gets lost in his own thoughts.

The first of the final three pages of ground-breaking *Green Lantern* #76. Writer: Denny O'Neal. Artist: Neal Adams. © DC Comics

THREE SET OUT TOGETHER, MOVING THROUGH CITIES AND VILLAGES AND THE MAJESTY OF THE WILDERNESS... SEARCHING FOR A SPECIAL KIND OF TRUTH... SEARCHING FOR THEMSELVES...

Acknowledgements

Thanks to the original, 1970 troupe of GRAFAN interviewers and friends: Bob Gale, the late Mike McFadden, the late Len McFadden and the late Bob Schoenfeld. Thanks also to Len for driving this kid around that crazy July day. (I only had my Learner's Permit.)

Thanks to *all* my GRAFAN club pals back then for creating and contributing to our meetings and zines, and for making it fun and mind-expanding to be a St. Louis comics and science-fiction enthusiast.

Thanks to long-time comic buddy and collaborator Don Secrease for cheering this book along and taking helpful peeks at it along the way. Couldn't have Don it without you, done! I mean, done it, Don!

Thanks to my wife Randy for understanding my recent, long hours away in the library, transcribing, formatting – and for my redundant comment at our nightly Sunset Sip™: "Yeah, I'm still working on that Denny O'Neil book."

Thanks to DC Comics for all the great reading moments; and for indulging the work I included here for academic study.

Thanks to the late artist Neal Adams, whose sketch of Denny for a DC house ad gave us an enlarged detail for this book's cover. Also, thanks just for being awesome.

Thanks to Denny O'Neil for the same.

Recommended Reading

Here's how to access some of the greatest comic stories
of Denny O'Neil and his collaborators from the era covered
in this book. Check Amazon or your Local Comics Shop.

Green Lantern / Green Arrow 1 (DC Comics, 2004)
Green Lantern and Green Arrow set out on a road trip to
rediscover America, finding racism, political corruption, and
capitalistic exploitation of workers.
Paperback | Kindle

Batman by Neal Adams Book Two (DC Comics, 2015)
Neal Adams' seminal Batman tales are collected in a new trade
paperback graphic novel series. This book includes many
Denny-scripted stories for *Batman* and *Detective*.
Paperback | Kindle

Showcase Presents: Bat Lash (DC Comics, 2009)
This volume stars Bat Lash, a self-professed pacifist, ladies' man
and gambler whose hands are never far from his six-guns.
Include the original stories from *Showcase* and *Bat Lash*.
Out-of-print paperback but available second-hand.

And you can still find Denny's non-fiction book available
in back-issue or second-hand venues, as well:

The DC Comics Guide to Writing Comics (DC Comics, 2001)
For any writer who wants to become an expert comic-book
storyteller, *The DC Comics Guide to Writing Comics* is a definitive
resource. In this valuable guide, Denny reveals his insider tricks
and no-fail techniques for comics storytelling.

About the Editor

Photo: Randy Rosenbaum

Walt Jaschek (left) is a St. Louis-based writer, editor, comic fan, and cosplayer of Dr. Henry ("Hank") Pym, the original Ant-Man, as seen in the Marvel Cinematic Universe – a subject not covered in this book. But we had to mention it.

He runs Walt Now Studios, an entertainment factory in St. Louis County, Missouri. His published comic works include Marvel's *What Th--?!; Recycled Man; Slightly Bent Comics;* and *The Golden Adventures of Brett Hull.*

Walt is currently writing a comedy screenplay about his high school years, the era in which this book's interview unfolded and many of Walt's teen-age misadventures ensued.

Maybe this book'll make it into the movie.

http://waltnow.com

Made in the USA
Columbia, SC
26 July 2024